Developing Creativity and Curiosity Outdoors

How to Extend Creative Learning in the Early Years

Julie Johnson and
Ann Watts

Routledge
Taylor & Francis Group

LONDON AND NEW YORK

First published 2019
by Routledge
2 Park Square, Milton Park, Abingdon, Oxon OX14 4RN

and by Routledge
711 Third Avenue, New York, NY 10017

Routledge is an imprint of the Taylor & Francis Group, an informa business

British Library Cataloguing in Publication Data
A catalogue record for this book is available from the British Library

Library of Congress Cataloging in Publication Data
Names: Johnson, Julie, 1962– author. | Watts, Ann, author.
Title: Developing creativity and curiosity outdoors : how to extend
creative learning in the early years / by Julie Johnson and Ann Watts.
Description: Abingdon, Oxon ; New York, NY : Routledge, 2018. |
Includes bibliographical references and index.
Identifiers: LCCN 2018002755| ISBN 9781138097209 (hbk) |
ISBN 9781138097216 (pbk) | ISBN 9781315105017 (ebk)
Subjects: LCSH: Science—Study and teaching (Early childhood)
—Activity programs. | Nature study—Activity programs. |
Outdoor education—Activity programs. | Curiosity in children. |
Creative ability in children.
Classification: LCC LB1139.5.S35 J64 2018 | DDC 372.35/044—dc23
LC record available at https://lccn.loc.gov/2018002755

ISBN: 978-1-138-09720-9 (hbk)
ISBN: 978-1-138-09721-6 (pbk)
ISBN: 978-1-315-10501-7 (ebk)

Typeset in Bembo
by Florence Production Ltd, Stoodleigh, Devon, UK

Contents

Foreword

Curiosity is an essential lifelong companion to any human life, if lost then the 'magic' of living and learning is lost. *Creativity and Curiosity Outdoors* is well-founded, well-researched and a wellspring of practical tips, resources and references for all practitioners who wish to exercise both their own creative muscles and those of their learners.

Imagination is our primary gift of human consciousness, we can review and revisit the past and, importantly, take on different views and show empathy – seeing with others' eyes and feeling with both others' and our own hearts. This infinite power of imagination in turn helps us predict and CREATE. Just last week, March 15th 2018, scientists published the most recent discoveries in East Africa demonstrating that humans were innovating about 320,000 years earlier than we previously thought – trading with distant groups, using colour pigments and manufacturing more sophisticated tools than those of the early stone age – helping humans survive unpredictable conditions. Our imagination and creativity are what make us human and will help us survive current unpredictable social and environmental situations.

This book, written by two experienced early years outdoor practitioners, takes us on a journey starting with a deep understanding of where creativity comes from, citing some well respected researchers and thinkers, from Vygotsky's notions on 'reproductive and creative activity' in child's pretend play, through to Professor Anna Craft's 'possibility thinking'.

Creativity is putting the imagination to work and in turn it feeds on imagination to bring ideas even more into the realm of the real. Ann and Julie give examples of how children apply their imagination and curiosity to the 'real' world, looking at the many facets that make up this human endeavor. They cite some clear case studies and approaches to stimulating and developing this basic part of being human. These include looking at how sensitive dialogue starting with "I wonder if …" questions can bring the imagination into sharp focus, through to how the hands can become the cutting edge of the mind in experiences such as breaking bark into a saucepan and mixing with crab apples to make apple pie. Sensitive resourcing and 'games' around fine and gross movements are outlined, being essential to brain and imaginative development. For where better to 'grow' than in the multi-sensory and 'healthy' outdoors? These form deep emotional memories on which to base imaginative thoughts and new creations.

Importantly this book gives a holistic view on how the outdoors can develop and integrate all that it is to be human and thoughtful in the outdoors with chapters on communication and storywork (for me 'the seat' of imagination); movement; craft; colour, shape and pattern; and sound and music.

If we are to innovate through this time of uncertainty, this type of education has to be some of the most important work we undertake, and indeed can be the most magical and gratifying.

Jon Cree, Director and founding chair of the
Forest School Association and Training Co-coordinator
for FSC Bishops Wood Centre, UK

Acknowledgements

Ann and Julie would like to express their grateful thanks to the staff, children and parents of the following early years settings:

Bus Stop Preschool

Crosfield Nursery School and Childrens Centre

Peter Pan Nursery and Forest School

Randolph Beresford Early Years Centre

Wild Learning Forest School – parent and toddler group and after school club.

Also to Jon Cree, Director and founding chair of the Forest School Association for his engaging and perceptive words in his Foreword.

Also to Jo Skone and staff at Randolph Beresford for the photographs of children and their art work in Chapter 7 and music in Chapter 8 and Charlotte Croucher for line drawings in Chapter 5.

And to the families of

Joshua, Harry and Lucy

Lucas and Henry

Martha

Steven

Wren and Jude.

About the authors

Julie Johnson's initial career and current voluntary work was in outdoor eduction youth work. Julie then trained in Early Years and Forest School and is the Forest School Manager at Peter Pan Nursery and Forest School, UK. Julie has been involved with the Open Sesame Project with Surrey and West Sussex and then the Creative Shoots Projects in Surrey. She is also Joint Chair of Forest School Association – Surrey Branch, UK.

Ann Watts initially trained as a teacher at Margaret McMillan College and this was the beginning of a career focused on outdoor education in the Early Years. She has had two nursery school headships where she was able to lead development of the outdoor spaces. She is now an Early Years Consultant, having also previously worked as an Early Years adviser for Surrey County Council, UK. Her previous publications include *Every Nursery Needs a Garden* (Routledge 2011), *Outdoor Learning through the Seasons* (Routledge 2013) and *Exploring Poetry with Young Children: Sharing and Creating Poems in the Early Years* (Routledge 2017).

Overview of the book

This book will offer inspiration to all adults who are involved with children in the Foundation Years. It focuses on how to encourage creativity in the outdoor environment. It is a response to the ever-increasing pressures on young children to conform to a more formal approach to education in this country, whereas children in Europe are free not only to enjoy their childhood but to learn the skills of self-confidence and creative thinking. There are exciting examples of good practice and in particular many ideas offered by Forest School. There are suggestions too of how to use these ideas in a wide variety of settings including those in an urban environment.

The book encourages adults to reflect on their own practice and be confident in letting children develop their own ideas. It gives examples of how to build on children's learning and encourage their imagination and curiosity.

Statement of aims

This book aims to:

- enable children from birth to five to develop their innate creativity and respond to the natural world with joy and imagination

- demonstrate how the Forest School approach supports creativity and how it can be adapted to suit a wide variety of settings

- inspire all adults who are involved with young children to use the natural environment in creative ways to support children's learning

- suggest five specific areas of creativity and how to develop them outdoors using the natural environment

- enable adults to reflect on their own practice and the nature of children's creative learning

- offer a relevant and up to date resource base for practitioners and researchers including practical suggestions and ideas, books, materials and internet information.

1 The nature of creativity

This first chapter of this book looks at some definitions of creativity and how it develops from birth onwards. It demonstrates how adults can support children to move from the present situation into one where there are many possibilities. The emotional relationship between adult and children is key to supporting children's creativity as they begin to experiment and explore ideas for themselves. There is further discussion about the role of children's imagination in creativity and what we mean by creativity skills.

It explores:

- theories of creativity in relation to learning and development in the early years
- the importance of emotional wellbeing in brain development and subsequent creativity
- the role of imagination and development of 'possibility thinking'
- the role of the adult as a Creative teacher
- what we mean by creative learners
- creative skills and why we need them.

Creativity – what is it?

The *Oxford English Dictionary* defines creativity as the 'ability to transcend traditional ideas rules and patterns and to create meaningful new ideas forms methods interpretations etc originality or imagination'. One online definition defines it as an act of transformation by which we turn one idea or thing into something else by way of intellectual chemical or manual alchemy . . . The sum of creativity is always greater than its parts. Creativity may look like a noun but it is really a verb – and in specific an action. It could be an interior or exterior process, – a thought or a manifestation, an idea or a product, but it is always an action, an energy, a putting one's self forth into the unknown. Creativity is the world of the intrepid explorer, of the adult two year old, who never ceases to ask the questions: Why? What if?

(www.creativityworkshop.com/whatiscreativity)

This definition puts us straight back into the world of the two-year-old and workshops run by this company often ask adults to think back to the time when they were children: 'We were all creative as children. We were creativity specialists before we learned to walk or talk. You never have to learn about your creativity from scratch – but you might need to reengage.'

Ironically, education through our own national curriculum will often stifle our originality so much that we can forget we were ever creative at all. Picasso seemed to reiterate this idea with his well-known statement: 'All children are artists. The problem is how to remain an artist once we grow up' (in Peter 1979, p. 25).

Contrary to our own current national curriculum, the curriculum for Scotland is based on creativity and there is a detailed and comprehensive report, 'Creativity Across Learning' published in 2013, which defines creativity as a 'process which generates ideas that have value to the individual. It involves looking at familiar things with a fresh eye examining problems with an open mind, making connections, learning from mistakes and using imagination to explore new possibilities' (Education Scotland 2013, p. 3).

This definition is well thought through and totally relevant for young children. It focuses on their thought processes and flow of ideas rather than any end product. It also uses the word 'imagination' and there will be an exploration of ideas on how this develops in very young children later in this chapter. The definition offered by the Thomas Coram centre in London states that creativity means 'connecting the previously unconnected in ways that are new and meaningful to the individual concerned to make real something you have imagined' (Duffy 2006).

Mel Rhodes (1961) identified the 'four Ps – Process, Product, Person and Place' and, more recently, the work of Kaufman and Beghetto introduces a 'four C' model of creativity (2009). They use the term 'mini c' to define the 'novel and personally meaningful interpretation of experiences, actions and events'. 'Little c' is the term applied to creative innovation in everyday activities available to the majority of people. 'Pro-c' describes the developmental progression beyond the last two that represents professional level expertise in any field and 'big C' is the term applied to what we may commonly refer to as a 'creative genius': that is someone who is eminent in their particular field.

This model has been explored further in connection with children's learning by Professor Anna Craft. She used the framework of 'big C' and 'little c' in her work with children and there is a section later in the chapter looking at her use of the term 'possibility thinking'.

Creativity – where does it start?

Brain development

Current research is using MRI scanning in very young children to examine the ways in which the human brain develops. Neuroscience is now able to map out the ways in which young brains make the connections that are the key to each child's individuality. Normal brain development is dependent upon environmental input and in particular warm, loving interactions with key adults, as well as a stimulating and appropriate environment for children to explore. Babies' brains continue to develop after birth. A baby's brain grows so much in the first three years of life that the head size needed to envelop it would not be able to pass down the birth canal. Consequently human babies are born earlier in their developmental cycle than most other mammals. This also has implications for the societal nature of our world. It means that children who receive the appropriate stimuli develop their speech patterns and language to reflect that of the adults around them. They develop taste preferences according to the kind of food they receive. They learn at a very early age how to attract the attention of adults and also how to communicate their needs. At the end of the first year a staggering 70 per cent of the adult brain size is in place and by the age of three around 90 per cent of the brain mass is in place. What is even more crucial is the nature of the development inside that brain mass.

The importance of emotional wellbeing in brain development

It follows that the experiences gained in the early years will have a fundamental effect on the way the brain develops. There is a powerful image published by Child Trauma Academy led by Bruce Perry MD PhD, which demonstrates the physical impacts of neglect on a child's brain. It shows the brain scan of a three-year-old who has been raised in a Romanian orphanage with very little if any sensory experience. The image sits next to the image of a healthy normal three-year-old and is significantly smaller in size. Malnutrition could be another factor but the researchers consider that the connectors in the brain have actually been pruned because of the lack of stimulating experiences (Early Arts 2017).

Although a baby's brain has around 100 billion neurons, evidence shows that only a quarter of the synaptic connections have been made. From birth until the age of three the young brain makes billions of new connections as knowledge is absorbed and children become more able to decode and make sense of the world around them. If the synapses are not connected, the under-used ones get pruned out so the connections that are used regularly get stronger and become more effective. There may be times later in life when these can be relearnt and this is referred to as a window of 'plasticity', but generally speaking it is in the first few years that the brain is able to develop its skills and competencies. This has major implications for the type and quality of experiences that adults offer to young children. 'By encouraging creativity and imagination we are promoting children's ability to explore and comprehend their world and increase their opportunities to make new connections and reach new understandings' (Duffy 2006).

The website www.zerotothree.org states that in the first three years the brain produces 700 new neural connections every second. Children's relationships with each other, the adults who care for them and the quality of their interaction with their surroundings, all play a crucial role in their development.

The development of creative activity

In his work, 'Imagination and creativity in childhood' (2004), Vygotsky states that people's behaviour falls into two basic categories. The first type is closely linked to memory and he calls this 'reproductive' behaviour or activity. This consists of reproducing or repeating previously developed behavioural patterns or resurrecting traces of earlier impressions. The second behavioural type he names 'creative activity'. This begins in the pretend play of young children and can be observed by what he refers to as object substitution. He gives the example of a young child using a stick as a horse. This is the beginning of imagination and it develops as the child internalises his language and thinking. In adolescence, it combines with conceptual thought and can reach its peak in adulthood through artistic, scientific and technological innovation.

CASE STUDY: MANAGING AND INITIATING LEARNING

W. aged 13 months came to stay overnight and while I was preparing lunch in the kitchen she crawled in to see me. I opened a cupboard door. She was immediately attracted by this and crawled to the space and proceeded to empty the cupboard of its contents, all plastic bowls, boxes and lids. She explored them in infinite detail putting a lid on her head and then sitting on another one. When she appeared to be losing interest after about ten minutes, I put a few wooden and plastic spoons on the floor and sat down with her and we experimented with different sounds as we banged on the boxes and the floor. Her concentration lasted for twenty minutes.

What was interesting, however, was that when she next came to visit a week later we were all in our sitting room but she immediately crawled away from us into the kitchen on her own and pulling herself up managed to open the cupboard door and proceeded to get out all the boxes. This was her activity of choice.

Babies have a natural curiosity and a need to explore.

W. is showing here what Vygotsky defines as reproductive activity which is closely linked to memory. As she gets older she will engage in creative activity which is defined as creating something new. It may be that she will use the same boxes, lids and sticks and make different sound patterns or start to build towers. She is currently at the stage of deconstruction which appears to precede construction. A row of sand pies several yards away on the beach will incite her to crawl rapidly towards them and systematically move along the line knocking them down. Deconstruction is a necessary stage of learning and precedes the constructive phase which adults often find easier to manage. Supporting children through deconstruction is difficult sometimes, as it seems to involve endless tidying up or repetitive play, as a toddler drops an object and waits for you to pick it up and return it. However with support, and through observation, children will learn how to begin to return objects, place blocks on top of each other or make a sand pie. This is the basic play that is an essential precedent to the development of creativity.

The role of imagination in developing creativity

Vygotsky (2004) shows that if the brain was only able to undertake this reproductive activity, a human being would be a creature who would adapt primarily to familiar stable conditions. A new or unexpected change not previously encountered would fail to induce the appropriate adaptive reactions. It is, therefore, essential that the brain is able to move on and develop what he refers to as combinatorial or creative activity. This involves the use of imagination. This orientates the human being towards the future. He believes that imagination as the oasis of all creative activity is an important component of absolutely all aspects of cultural life, and it enables both scientific and technical as well as artistic creation.

Einstein (1931) emphasises that imagination is more important than knowledge. He feels knowledge is limited to what we know and understand, whereas imagination can embrace the world and everything in it. Imagination is the ability to form a picture in your mind of something that is not real or that you have not seen before. It is inextricably linked with creativity and also with creative thinking as children use their developing imaginations to help them make sense of the real world and also to explore new and exciting ideas and possibilities. Role play, as we call it, is very evident in the second year of play. Children are able to use object substitution but some can put themselves into imaginary situations, maybe assuming the role of a parent, a doctor or a fireman in their play. They are modelling behaviour and as their language patterns develop they often assume the speech patterns to fit in with this role. This is an essential stage in the development of creative thinking and as practitioners we need to be aware of the importance of this type of play.

Creative thinking is dependent upon imagination and in turn imagination will extend and develop creative thinking. This is shown in the following case study:

CASE STUDY: THE ICE CREAM SHOP

Children at Randolph Beresford Early Years Centre chose ice cream scoops from their resource base and decided to create an ice cream shop. They collected some larger containers and used spoons to fill them with earth. They then mixed the earth with pebbles, small stones and ladled it out into smaller containers. Each child appeared to be making a different flavour. H. was making blue ice cream and A. bought some and paid with 'leaf money'. H. carefully counted it out and he ran off with the leaves, climbed a ladder onto a small roof and sorted the leaves carefully away. 'The till's up here'.

The play was extended because an adult was present supporting children by offering resources and encouraging them to find their own. Large ivy leaves were used to make cones and children carefully placed the mixture on the leaf. The children then ran off to create a train placing logs end to end. H. was the driver. 'We're going to London Beach.' 'There's a monster in the tunnel.' H. jumped out of the train and other children followed him as he ran around for a while before returning to the train. Not all the children returned to the train and H. continued to develop his theme, filling his car with petrol and then returning to the ice cream shop to buy ice cream for his family.

(A. = Adult, H. = child)

Creative thinking depends on imagination and H. was able to make ice cream and then extend his play to include a train trip and then return for more ice cream for his 'family'

Creative thinking in young children

Anna Craft has written extensively on the subject of creativity in young children. She coined the term 'possibility thinking' and also referred frequently to the distinction between what she calls 'big C' and 'little c' creativity (Craft 2002). She defined possibility thinking as 'the transition from "What is" to "what might be"'. By observing and listening to the children in our care we encourage their questions, their thinking and their imaginative play. Children's ideas are taken seriously and best practice encourages them to develop these ideas. Often both children and adults are unsure of the outcome but the sense of satisfaction and achievement when a satisfactory outcome is reached is a positive benefit in the development of children's self-confidence and self-esteem. She stated that any pedagogy which nurtures possibility thinking is characterised by the quality of the relationships between adults and children. Adults enable children to become involved and they will offer children time and space to explore ideas. Creative thinking involves the use of the creative skills and is the process by which we come up with a new idea. It may happen individually or as part of a group. Adults and children alike will need to share ideas when embarking on a group task. Very often the ideas of one person can act as a springboard for the ideas of another. The process can be deliberate or accidental. Ongoing creative thinking

CASE STUDY: RANDOLPH BERESFORD EARLY YEARS CENTRE

The water slide

M. *chose a mallet from the resource box and set off to find some short sticks. She chose some of similar length and with some adult support banged them upright into the ground. She used string to enclose them. 'I'm making a house.' She ran back to the cabin to collect wooden figures. 'These are the family.' She picks up another stick. 'That's the table.'*

A. *'Do we need any more furniture? We've got a table.'*

M. *'A bed.'*

R. *arrives and begins to strike the house as if to knock it down. The adult intervenes and asks M. 'Do you want him to knock it down?' She shakes her head. 'Then you must ask him not to.'*

M. *[to R.] 'I don't want you to do that R.'*

A. *[to R.] 'You can build your own house and knock it down if you like.'*

He *leaves and M. continues by placing a very damp stick outside the structure.*

M. *'This is the water slide.'*

A. *'How can you make it better?'*

M. *'We need some water.'*

She runs to the tap and puts a wheel barrow under it. Other children join her and they try to fill it, not noticing it has a leak and water is escaping. M pushes it back to the mound but can't get it up the hill as there is a long plank in the way.

She runs to the plank and lifts it up and puts it on her head to balance it. 'I need some help.'

Other children join in to hold the plank and the adult is left to push the barrow up. They tip the remaining water onto the stick to complete the slide.

A supportive adult nearby enabled this extended creative problem solving to reach a satisfactory conclusion as the plank was removed so the wheelbarrow could get up the mound to supply the water for the slide.

(A. = adult, M. = child, R. = child)

is the continuous investigation, questioning and analysis that develop through education training and self-awareness. Every child has creative potential and is capable of creative expression in some form. It does depend on the appropriate involvement of adults who understand and are able to foster this process.

What is creative learning?

This term describes the 'range of activities and processes undertaken by an individual which supports the development of creativity and other skills' (Education Scotland 2013).

According to a collection of essays published by Demos in 2010, *Born Creative* (Tims 2010), children who have been exposed to creative learning in Early Years Education are the key to a prosperous modern economy. They argue that young children who access creative learning are more likely to succeed in adult life by developing the skills they need to perform in the work place or wider society as entrepreneurs and citizens. The subtitle to this collection is 'Creative learning in the early years is not just child's play'. In the introduction to these essays, Penny Egan highlights the fact that all the essays start with the premise that children's creativity is a matter of public concern. Loughton and Teather (2010) argue, in the second essay, that promoting creativity and play is a first class ticket to producing a creative prosperous economy many years down the line. We are already eight years down the line and the focus on children's learning seems to be increasingly targeted on goals and achievements within the mathematical and literacy framework. Play is becoming marginalised and with some notable exceptions, many children from the age of five or even four in reception classes spend much of their time in adult-directed tasks rather than engaging in challenging problem solving and play opportunities.

The last essay in this collection, by Shirley Brice Heath (2010) places emphasis on the fact that children are natural explorers but need to be in the right environment to be creative. Finding spaces and places that foster imagination and creativity is becoming more difficult. Practitioners need to be creative and imaginative in their approach to the spaces that are accessible and this book will suggest ways of using outdoor spaces in this way. They also need to give children time and space. They need to stand back sufficiently to observe what motivates intrigues, confuses or inspires the children they are working with. Studies on possibility thinking (Cremin, Burnard and Craft 2006) all emphasis the quality of the relationship between adults and children. There are case studies in this book which demonstrate that it is the nature of the relationship between adults and children that supports emotional development and in turn gives the child the confidence to explore and test ideas and theories. The following case study does just this, as well as showing how the adult also steps back occasionally and lets the children sort out the problem for themselves.

This study shows the maturity and levels of understanding of two children. The younger child knows what he wants to do, but does not quite understand how to do it. The older child knows exactly what needs to be done, but has the maturity level to understand that the activity was started by the younger child and he should offer help but not interfere or take over the activity. The role of the adult was to support by providing additional materials that could be useful and not making any judgements or suggestions on how the task could be achieved. It is interesting that the children, although they didn't complete the task, were still satisfied with their achievement.

CASE STUDY: MOVING THE TROLLEY

F. became obsessed with the small trolley, which was used by the children to carry their own tools. It had two ropes which two children needed to negotiate when getting through small gaps or over logs.

During a particularly wet time of year, pulling the trolley through every puddle fascinated this child. The practitioners changed the central camp to an area that had an island which was now surrounded with water. They were interested in seeing what the child would do within this new area. Straight away he emptied out the contents of the trolley and rolled it into the water, still holding the ropes, saying he was going to get it to the island. He was given some longer bits of rope to tie to the trolley and with a little help tied it on. By now he had the interest of another child, D. Together they talked about getting the trolley over to the island. D. understood that he would need to push the trolley out, but F. was still pushing the trolley, but then pulling on the rope. D. said they needed a stick, and found a long one, which they used together to push the trolley further towards the island. F. then picked up the rope and pulled on it, still not understanding that his actions were making the task more difficult. It took several attempts before F. realized that by pulling on the rope he was undoing all the work they had done with the stick. What was really surprising to the adults was that D. was allowing F. to continue with his own ideas without any argument, although he repeatedly said, 'We need to push not pull', and would go and find longer sticks with other children. The children didn't quite make their goal, but each of them was satisfied with what they did achieve. F. then made a suggestion to the adult: 'We need to get a boat!'

(F. child aged 3 years 8 months, D. child aged 4 years 6 months)

'Let's try a small stick.'

'Here's a bigger one.'

'Pushing or pulling?'

The role of the adult – creative teaching

Developing creativity depends firstly, on building a warm and trusting relationship between adults and children, where children feel safe and can trust the adult. They need to be given time and space to explore their own ideas. The adult also needs to relax and allow his or her own creative resources and skills to come into play. This may be done through providing exciting resources, maybe using natural resources in a new and imaginative way. It could also be done through asking exciting and challenging questions or just gently floating an idea. Each curriculum section of this book will offer suggestions of ideas and resources to inspire adults to develop their own creativity.

Children's creative abilities can be related to their developmental stages. It is important to put the emphasis on the creative process rather than the product or outcome which may result. Malaguzzi (1993) feels that creativity is more visible when adults are more interested in the way children approach things cognitively than in the results they actually achieve.

Creative teaching can encourage children's imaginations. It can be in the form of story making, role play, building a shelter, catching imaginary fish with a stick and a piece of string, listening to birdsong and wondering what the bird is singing about. It may involve music making in many forms, creating an installation or design from natural materials or using words to create a poem.

Using a stick as a fishing rod, this child is totally involved and happy

Developing the relationship between emotional wellbeing and creativity

Sandra Russ (1996) has developed a model which explains the relationship between psychological processes and creativity. She suggests three factors are involved.

The first is the personality of the child and their level of self-confidence, curiosity, motivation and ability to tolerate ambiguity. This is followed by the emotional processes such as pleasure in challenge and risk taking, tolerance of anxiety and emotional fantasy in play. This is succeeded by the cognitive abilities, such as sensitivity to problems, breadth of knowledge and judgement and ability to transform thinking. She suggests that children need a combination of all these in order to be creative. The role of the adult is therefore to observe the level of each component and support and encourage areas which may not be so evident. Observation is key and the adult will need to reflect on ways to encourage either the self-confidence of an anxious child, or extend thinking processes and encourage imagination and curiosity in another. Her later research (Russ 2003) focuses on the importance of play, and in particular role play and the role of imagination, insights into problem solving and the ability to experience emotion and make choices. Dealing with some stress builds a strong brain. Helpful stress helps us learn to solve problems and manage feelings. If the adult is there to support, a child is more able to tolerate stress and to relate to others.

Shonkoff and Phillips (2000) demonstrate that high quality social and cultural experiences are critical in the early years for healthy brain development and well-rounded personalities. Children are active participants in their own development, reflecting the intrinsic human drive to explore and master one's environment. Again Shonkoff and Phillips stress the importance of human relationships and the effects of these on children's development. Creative teachers will provide a balance between structure and freedom of expression. They will plan adult-led activities but also observe the children and find what interests and motivates them. They will encourage children to develop their own ideas. Problem solving will be encouraged and children supported to negotiate and work both on their own and with their peers. They will need to be flexible in their own thinking and able to adapt and utilise situations and opportunities as they arise. The work of Julie Fisher (2016) offers a clear exposition of the nature of interaction with children and demonstrates the difference between interfering and interacting. This is shown too in the case study in Chapter 9 where the adult responds to the different interests of children in the group and allows them to make their own discoveries.

In addition there may be occasions where children can work alongside artists, scientists or musicians. Children in the Reggio Emilia preschools are encouraged to use drawing as a graphic language. Their indoor spaces are planned so there is plenty of space for free movement and physical expression. Spaces are rich in resources and tools for the children to use.

Questions have been raised as to whether as a society we are becoming so risk averse that we are stifling creative opportunity for our children. The richness of experience of the early year's curriculum in many settings in England cannot be favourably compared with that enjoyed by children in other European countries, in particular in Scandinavia. Scotland has a wider range of opportunity and there are some nursery schools that operate a full outdoor curriculum all through the year. However it is in the early years settings where we are able to have enough autonomy to provide what we know children need and it becomes crucial that all settings are able to meet this challenge. So many children when they reach Key Stage 1 are subject to the confines of a curriculum dedicated to outcomes and rigid targets.

What are creativity skills and why do we need them?

The Scottish government has identified four core creativity skills which apply across the curriculum. It defines creativity skills as those skills which 'contribute to an individual's capacity to understand and define a creative process'.

Creativity is at the heart of the Scottish curriculum and is fundamental to the definition of what it means to be a 'successful learner' in the Scottish education system.

They offer statements under the four main headings: Curiosity, Open mindedness, Imagination and Problem solving. As these are so clearly set out and particularly relevant to working with very young children, they are included below (Education Scotland 2013, *Creativity Across Learning 3–18*, p. 5).

Curiosity

Learners are constructively inquisitive and can demonstrate this by:

- being curious

- registering patterns and anomalies

- making use of previous knowledge

- researching productively

- formulating good questions.

Open mindedness

Learners are open to new ideas and can demonstrate this by:

- using lateral thinking

- using divergent thinking

- hypothesising

- exploring multiple view points

- being flexible, adaptable and functioning with uncertainty.

Imagination

Learners are able to harness their imagination and can demonstrate this by:

- exploring, synthesising and refining multiple options

- generating and refining ideas

- inventing.

Problem solving

Learners are able to identify and solve problems and can demonstrate this by:

- understanding and defining problems

- crafting, delivering and presenting solutions demonstrating initiative, discipline, persistence and resilience

- evaluating impact and success of solutions.

Creative learners will be:

- motivated and ambitious for change for the better, including their own capabilities

- confident in the value of their own viewpoint

- able to apply a creative process to other situations

- able to lead and work well with others.

How can adults encourage the development of these skills?

All the thought processes that lead to creativity depend on imagination. Children need to be in the right environment to be creative and this is important from birth onwards. The importance of a warm and loving relationship with a primary carer cannot be underestimated. This helps the baby's brain to develop and make neural connections. This happens at an astonishing rate and by the age of 18 months some children are beginning to develop their imagination and move from what Vygotsky calls reproductive activity to combinatorial or creative activity. The implications for adults spending time with young children whether at home or in a nursery setting are very profound. The way we observe and respond to the children has a significant effect on their development. By regarding ourselves as creative partners with the children we can embark on an exciting journey with them. Often the children will take the lead and how the adults respond to this will have a profound influence on the nature of the children's emotional wellbeing and their learning.

There are two parts to the creative process. The first is the beginning of an idea which may or may not be shared with others. This may take time and it is important to allow children time to ponder over a situation. After an incubation period, ideas may become more concrete as children begin to use their imagination and their thought processes. They may be working in a group or on their own. Adults need to observe and participate in the process, sometimes as a negotiator, an encourager, or a motivator. It may be possible to ask the questions, 'what might happen if you . . .?' or 'what might happen if . . . ?' Creative learning involves investigating, discovering, inventing and cooperating. Rosen (2010, p. 11) says at least one of these will be present in any creative learning experiences. Ideally it will be all four.

Adults need to support children in their own reflections on what they are doing but also need to allow time to reflect on their own practice. 'What went really well today?' 'Should I have handled that differently?' 'What could I do better?' The points for discussion at the end of each chapter can be also used as a starting point as you consider how best to give children the opportunities they deserve and need.

Conclusion

If adults are questioned about creativity, they may well respond with reference to art, music or drama. The 'arts', as we call them, depend on what we generally refer to as creative people – the big C people. However, we can see from the definitions in this chapter that creativity embraces all aspects of our thinking and is something inherent in everyone.

Bloom's (1956) taxonomy encourages us to think about the inclusiveness of creativity. 'What is more creative than good science, technology and mathematics? Expert scientists, technologists and mathematicians are no less creative than talented artists or creative writers.'

The debate which was raised in England at the beginning of this century already appears to have been marginalised. This is in direct contrast to Scotland where the debate appears to be gathering momentum and where creativity is placed firmly at the heart of learning. This chapter concludes with a further reference to the Curriculum for Excellence. In 2013 Education Scotland published a report entitled *Creativity across Learning 3–18*.

They recognise that the ability to think creatively is one of the most important tools in helping children to develop higher order skills to enable them to thrive in an uncertain social and economic climate. They acknowledge that there is international support for the idea that developing creativity skills helps people to learn better whatever the subject area. There are clear links between this aspect of creativity and the development of critical thinking skills.

In the foreword to the report Bill Maxwell highlights three recurring themes. The first of the key themes is the need to help children take greater responsibility for planning their own learning. The next theme focuses on the need to establish open ended approaches to learning. This is akin to the 'What if? What happens next?' approach to learning suggested by Anna Craft. Thirdly, he highlights the need to use external partnerships and stimuli to broaden and enhance the learning experience.

The philosophy of the Forest School movement which also encompasses these ideas will be discussed in more detail in Chapter 3, as we highlight and reflect on ways in which this can be used in all settings to enrich the imagination and the learning journeys of our children.

This book aims to encourage adults to respond to the natural world around them and to encourage children to respond, using all our senses as we embark on journeys of which we will never know the end. By supporting children's creativity and encouraging their creative learning we will hopefully enable them to acquire the skills which they need to participate and thrive in adult life. We need to hold firm to our beliefs that children learn through play. Carl Jung (1992) stated that the creative mind plays with the object it loves. He feels that the creation of something new is not accomplished by the intellect but by the play instinct arising from inner necessity (para 197).

We need to articulate our beliefs that creativity needs to be encouraged and not stifled during the primary and secondary school years. Emotional wellbeing, self-confidence and self-esteem will result in children being able to develop their imagination and show curiosity, offer ideas, negotiate, solve problems and reflect on their thinking. 'Educators who rise to the creativity challenge will be well rewarded in rich teaching experiences and the joy of seeing children reach their creative potential in supportive and integrated learning systems' (O'Connor 2012).

We need to develop creativity through learning and in turn learn through creativity.

POINTS FOR DISCUSSION

- Are all practitioners aware of the need for creative practice? How can you develop this understanding and ensure that adults are aware of the importance of this?

- What steps do you take to establish a warm and trusting relationship with all children as they begin their life at nursery? Are there ways you could improve this?

- Discuss what is meant by 'possibility thinking'. How can you transform situations from 'What is?' to 'What might be?'

- Do all adults give children space and time to develop their own ideas? How can you further support children to do this?

- Consider the role of the adults in the two case studies. How do they support the child in making discoveries for themselves?

- Are adults in your setting able to reflect and share their own practice with each other?

USEFUL RESOURCES

These books and websites are a valuable resource for anyone wanting to explore the nature of creativity in more depth.

Bringing the Reggio Emilia Approach to your Early Years Practice by Linda Thornton and Pat Brunton (Routledge 2014) – A clear account of the principles of the Reggio Approach and how it links to our own EYFS and how to build in this creativity into your own setting.

Cultivating Creativity in Babies Toddlers and Young Children, 2nd edition, by Tina Bruce (Hodder Education 2011)

Creative Learning 3–11 and How We Document It, edited by Anna Craft and Teresa Cremin (Trentham Books 2008)

Creativity and Creative Pedagogies in the Early and Primary Years by Teresa Cremin (Routledge 2016) – An interesting collection of writings from different countries of the world revealing the complex nature of creative pedagogy together with perspectives on the tensions between the need for creative teaching and the restrictions offered by accountability curricula.

Creativity Education and Society, writings of Anna Craft (Trentham Books 2015)

'Promote Creativity and Creative Learning in Young Children', Unit CYPOP7 (Hodder Education 2014, can be found as a pdf file online at https://www. hoddereducation.co.uk/getmedia/17883c9c-3cf8-4c1a-9a58-8de37f5ed2a1/ CHAPTER-22.aspx) – This pdf file is designed as a unit in the Children and Young People's workforce diploma, and is a useful starting point for adults who want to learn more about creativity.

The Hundred Languages of Children by Carolyn Edwards, the Reggio Emilia Experience in Transformation (Greenwood Press 2011) – A collection of writings offering a deeper insight into the 'Hundred Languages' with photographs from the schools in Reggio Emilia.

Doing Your Early Years Research Project: A Step by Step Guide by Guy Roberts-Holmes (Sage 2005) – a useful starting point for anyone thinking about a research project – why not consider writing about creativity?

www.creativityworkshop.com/whatiscreativity

www.creativeeducation.co.uk

www.demos.uk *Born Creative a series of essays* 2010

www.educationscotland.gov.uk *Curriculum for Excellence/creativity* 2010

www.zerotothree.org

Bibliography

Bloom, B.S. (Ed.). Engelhart, M.D., Furst, E.J., Hill, W.H., and Krathwohl, D.R. (1956) Taxonomy of Educational Objectives, Handbook I: *The Cognitive Domain*. New York: David McKay Co. Inc.

Brice Heath, S. (2010) 'Play in Nature: the foundation of creative thinking', in C. Tims (ed.), *Born Creative*. Available online at https://www.demos.co.uk/project/born-creative/.

Craft, A. (2002) '"Little c" creativity', in A. Craft, B. Jeffrey and M. Leibling (eds), *Creativity in Early Years Education: A Lifewide Foundation*. London: Continuum.

Cremin, T., Burnard, P. and Craft, A. (2006) 'Pedagogy and possibility thinking in the early years', *Thinking Skills and Creativity*, 1(2).

Duffy, B. (2006) *Creativity and Imagination in the Early Years*. Maidenhead: Open University Press.

Early Arts (2017) 'Creativity in Early Brain Development', blog, 30 March. Available at: https://earlyarts.co.uk/blog/creativity-in-early-brain-development.

Education Scotland (2013) *Creativity across Learning 3–18*. Available at: https://education.gov.scot/improvement/Documents/Creativity/CRE1_WhatAreCreativitySkills/Creativity3to18.pdf.

Einstein, A. (1931) *Cosmic Religions: With Other Opinions and Aphorisms*. New York: Covici Friede.

Fisher, J. (2016) *Interacting or Interfering? Improving Interactions in the Early Years*. London: Open University Press.

Jung, C.G. (1992) *The Collected Works of C. G. Jung, Vol.6: Psychological Types*. London: Routledge.

Kaufman, J.C. and Beghetto, R.A. (2009) 'Beyond Big and Little C: The four C model of Creativity', *Review of General Psychology*, 13(1): 1–12.

Loughton, T. and Teather, S. (2010) 'Creating the Conditions: trusted professional and targeted resources for creativity in the early years', in C. Tims (ed.) *Born Creative*. Available online at https://www.demos.co.uk/project/born-creative/.

Malaguzzi, L. (1993) 'History, ideas and basic philosophy: an interview with Lella Gandini', in C. Edwards, L. Gandini and G. Forman (eds), *The Hundred Languages of Children: The Reggio Emilia Approach, Advanced Reflections*, second edition. Greenwich: Ablex Publishing.

O'Connor, D. (2012) 'Creativity in Childhood: The Role of Education', conference presentation at 8th Global Conference: Creative Engagements Thinking with Children. Available at: www.researchonline.nd.edu.au/edu_conference/76/.

Peter, L.J. (1979) *Ideas for our Time*. New York: Bantam Books.

Rhodes, M. (1961) 'An analysis of creativity', *The Phi Delta Kappan* 42(7): 305–310.

Rosen, M. (2010) 'Foreword', in C. Tims (ed.), *Born Creative*. Available online at https://www.demos.co.uk/project/born-creative/.

Russ, S.W. (1996) 'Development of creative processes in children', in M.A. Runco (ed.), *Creativity from Childhood through Adulthood: Developmental Issues* (New Directions for Child Development No. 72). San Francisco CA: Jossey-Bass.

Russ, S.W. (2003) 'Play and creativity: developmental issues', *Scandinavian Journal of Educational Research* 47(3): 291–303.

Shonkoff, J. and Phillips, D.A. (eds) (2000) *From Neurons to Neighbourhoods: The Science of Early Childhood Development*. Washington DC: National Academies Press.

Tims, C. (ed.) (2010) *Born Creative*. Available online at https://www.demos.co.uk/project/born-creative/.

Vygotsky, L.S. (2004) 'Imagination and creativity in childhood', *Journal of Russian and East European Psychology* 42(1): 7–97.

2 The nature of curiosity and imagination

This chapter examines the nature of curiosity and imagination and explores the role of the adult in encouraging and developing this in babies and young children. Adults need to establish a strong emotional relationship with the children, provide an exciting and challenging environment and support and extend children's thinking and ideas. The chapter shows how imagination and curiosity are an integral part of all the characteristics of effective learning as stated in the UK as part of the Foundation Stage guidelines for adults working with children of this age.

The chapter discusses:

- the nature of curiosity
- the nature of imagination
- ways to develop outdoor spaces
- the role of the adult in questioning, sharing and extending
- loose parts play
- characteristics of effective learning.

The nature of curiosity

Babies have a natural instinct to explore and there is a need to keep them safe as they begin to use their mouths as well as their hands and feet. They will experiment as soon as they are able to exercise some degree of muscle control and once they start moving, adults are again challenged to keep them safe.

At the same time, however, it is important to encourage this developing sense of exploration and curiosity. Outdoors offers an even more exciting and stimulating environment and by taking very young babies outside from a very young age we are encouraging them to develop their senses.

As they get older and begin to crawl and walk, exploration becomes the main focus of their existence. It is vital that adults are aware of the need to encourage this and encourage the child to make discoveries for himself.

They will hear a range of sounds and be able to hear and see leaves blowing in the breeze.

Exciting new environments encourage curiosity and concentration in very young children

Friedrich Froebel (1887) believed that teachers should help children make their own discoveries. According to Froebelian philosophy a 'thirsty plant' is a metaphor for the natural curiosity of the young child. He realised that curiosity was children's leading asset and he recommended that they invent problems as well as just solving them. He highlighted that passive listening leaves children in a passive state and sustained interest required some degree of action on their part (Hughes 1910).

This philosophy is reflected in what is now referred to in the United Kingdom as the Characteristics of Effective Learning. Each of the three main headings has three subheadings, all of which highlight the need for adults to offer children rich and stimulating learning experiences where children can become involved at the deepest level. The role of the adult is, therefore, to offer an exciting environment; to observe how children respond and then to interact; to offer suggestions to stimulate the child's curiosity; to offer reassurance where necessary and lots of praise and encouragement.

Encouraging children to ask questions is one of the most important things we can do. However it is also important that we respond to these questions appropriately for this is the bedrock of a developing and curious mind. This is where we lay the foundations for the way the child responds to others and to the world around him. 'The important thing is not to stop questioning. Curiosity has its own reason for existence' (Einstein 1955, p. 64).

'Why' and 'How' are two of the most important words that a young child learns. Children with limited language development often find it hard to ask questions and we need to observe, not only whether children are able to ask questions, but the complexity of their questions.

How do we respond?

Young children are probably the most determined seekers for answers amongst mankind. Anyone who has had a small toddler will recall the endless stream of questions that can be asked within a short space of time. Adults need to be honest in their responses and recognise that children will develop their attitudes and dispositions towards learning through the nature of our response. If we offer a simple short answer, we are not developing the child's desire to explore. However, if we respond, with maybe another question or a longer explanation, that may stimulate the child to want to know more.

An example might be if a child asks, 'How many legs does a spider have?' Instead of offering the correct answer outright, encourage the child to find the answer. If possible use a magnifying glass to look at a real spider. If not, use a picture book and then continue the exploration by using questions such as 'Look, some legs are bigger and some spiders have hairy legs. What do they use their legs for?'

This could lead on to an extended conversation about how a spider can spin a web and in turn a conversation about the food chain.

The nature of imagination

Imagination is more important than knowledge, for knowledge is limited to all we now know and understand, while imagination embraces the whole world and all there will be to know and understand.

Albert Einstein (n.d.)

We cannot ever know what a baby is actually thinking, but as a child gets older we can see an emerging pattern of fantasy and imagination in their play. A child as young as fifteen months will demonstrate, through play, the beginnings of imaginary thinking as they pick up a phone and hold it to their ear. A responsive adult will respond and encourage a conversation even though the child may not be using recognisable language. Repeated sounds often occur. Similarly children begin to act out familiar scenes they have seen at home. Role play in the home corner will show very young children pretending to cook a meal, sweep the floor, sit down at the table and eat pretend food. A child of eighteen months will demonstrate that she can care for her dolly as a mother might care for a baby. She will use a pretend bottle or a small spoon to feed the doll as she wraps it up and takes it out in the pushchair. As imagination develops, children between the age of two and three may well use a different object to represent something else: e.g. a wooden block instead of a toy telephone. Their imagination is sufficiently developed to imbue an object with different features to accord with their play needs. For example a wooden stick may be a fishing rod, a drumstick, cutlery, a sweeping brush or even a toothbrush.

Natural materials can be used in a multitude of ways as the complexity of play develops. James Gibson (1986) describes this as the theory of 'affordance'.

The short case study on the facing page illustrates this, as well as showing how natural materials enable children to concentrate for long periods of imaginative play.

It shows how children will use what is available and adapt resources to meet their play needs. Their imagination does the rest.

The child with the saucepan was completely involved for a sustained period of time, and met the criteria for level 5 of high involvement on the Leuven involvement scales. These scales, devised by Ferre Laevers, indicate that children who operate at levels 4 and 5 show that learning is taking place at a deeper level. It is thought that unless pupils are operating at levels 4 or 5 learning will be limited.

By the age of three, children are moving into imaginary worlds as they listen to stories about the Gruffalo and other imaginary creatures. They will use a range of materials to construct a fire engine, an aeroplane or rocket and enact their own imaginary dramas. By the age of four many children are ready to venture forward into mythical worlds of dragons, fairies and imaginary creatures, whether of their own making or part of a complex story or play that can be introduced by an adult.

By encouraging children to use their imagination, adults are supporting children to use their creative thinking skills. This can be done through the use of story and language as children discuss and invent make believe scenarios. Working outdoors, they will be able to use natural materials to make fairy homes, a castle for a prince or a giant. As children develop more complex language

CASE STUDY: MAKING APPLE PIE

In the mud kitchen at the Bus Stop Nursery there are clearly defined areas. In the centre of the floor four logs mark out a square and within this is a cooking pot with a metal grid on top. There are logs for children to sit on.

One child was busy breaking up small pieces of bark and putting them into a small saucepan on top of the metal grid. She occasionally stirred it up using a long cane. Staff observed that she left the pan while she went to the toilet and asked another child to look after it together with the long stirring stick. She returned and continued with this activity for another period of around fifteen minutes. Nearby another child had gathered up some small crab apples and put them in the large washing up bowl in the sink. She added some small pieces of bark and announced she was making apple pie. She picked up a paper cupcake case and sprinkled it over the bowl. 'That's the sugar', she announced. She was asked if she was going to cook the pie and replied, 'no it's a hot day, it's going to be cold'.

Cooking apple pie – natural materials can be used to encourage concentration and deep involvement in play

Two boys came up to investigate the apple pie situation. Both were holding some small twigs. Observation showed that these twigs were not random but had been carefully chosen. A. held three long thin twigs, one being much longer than the others. He announced that they were his dinosaurs and that the one with a long neck was a brontosaurus. R. held a selection of twigs that were flatter and smaller in shape. 'These are dinosaur fossils.'

and patterns of thought, so their imaginations will develop. Adults can encourage this by ensuring that stories and play themes are within the child's understanding. Some children however may come to a nursery setting with limited experiences of play and adults will need to support these children, maybe offering additional messy play experiences, realistic human figures and a range of toy items such as boats so they begin to understand how to build these into play. They need this realistic understanding to enable them to move on into imaginary play, maybe using sticks as figures or bark and leaves to make boats.

CASE STUDY: FINDING THE TIN TREASURE IN THE 'CROCODILE'

Setting the scene

At a woodland site, children have gone over to the old fallen tree. This has been known by the children as the Crocodile. Last year's children introduced this concept to them during their induction to Forest School sessions, and it has remained with them.

Two boys are playing around the fallen tree 'crocodile' structure; one boy is hammering using a mallet, the other has been collecting natural materials using one of the lidded containers in the children's tool trolley; he is using this as 'medicine' for the crocodile.

Child 1 W. – 'Make sure he don't eat it' – talking to the other child, as he has just broken off some small pieces of bark.

Child 2 F. – Continues hammering and moving collected materials around the fallen tree structure. 'You need to put it in his tummy, this is his tummy.'

He continues with his hammering and then moves around the structure and then finds a blue tin within the tree structure, very excited that the crocodile has left a present for them. 'Look, look a little present, the crocodile left a present.'

W. – 'Wow, look guys' (taking present from F.), running, tripping but picking himself up quickly to continue running towards the other children.

F. – repeating – 'A little present, look, a present – cookies.'

Both running with the tin, to the other children in the group, who are playing on the hammock, to show them the tin.

Once there, they open the tin, and immediately try to eat some of the contents.

W. – 'Look the crocodile gave us these.'

M. – 'Wow.'

I. – smiling, then says, 'Are they just pretend?'

F. – takes one to try, licks it, smells it.

M. – 'What are those?'

N. – takes one – 'Yuck it's like playdough.'

Adult – 'I don't think I'm going to eat them, it looks like they might be for something else.'

There is then a conversation around what they were made of, the patterns on them and then why they were there. One child felt it was because they were good, another child thought the crocodile might leave more presents for them. One child thought it was made like playdough, another thought it might be food for the crocodile.

Finding treasure in the crocodile

The boys felt the need to share this news with the rest of the group who were listening to them and eager to see what it is inside the tin. One child is matter of fact, explaining, 'It's just pretend'. The added treasure provoked a new line of enquiry for the children.

Make believe games are the forerunners of self-regulation. Children take on roles and learn social skills such as communication, problem solving and empathy (Hughes 2010). Forward planning on the part of the practitioners encourages children's imagination in this way and this in turn strengthens friendship bonds and communication between the children. They also have a strong emotional connection to the imaginary crocodile and are very serious in their efforts to help him feel better.

Three boys on a Forest School session in an unstructured time for play and exploration discovered a circular hollow in the ground full of leaves. One lay down on his back and kicked his legs to move the leaves. 'You're swimming', said another. 'This is our swimming pool.'

They all lay down and made swimming movements. One climbed out and stood on the edge.

'This is our diving board.'

He 'dived' in.

They developed this theme by adding some logs to the diving board area to raise it and continued to play for some time as a group.

There was a complicit understanding within this group of how to extend their own play and they were able to use the natural materials around to enable them to do this.

Adult questions and speculations

The questions asked by adults should encourage and extend conversations and discussions, e.g. 'Who or what might be living inside that tree stump?' or 'Did you hear that sound over there, what could it be?' These will allow children to give a wide variety of answers or extend the imagination. If adults can enter into the imaginary world of the children they will be able to extend the play by the use of 'provocations' such as leaving the tin of cookies by the 'crocodile' in the case study above. This is discussed further in Chapters 4 and 5.

Design and layout of space

Small spaces for small world play can be added to corners and some imagination on the part of the adults will encourage children to engage in imaginative play. Use tarpaulins and fabrics to create dens and shelters. A gravel and rock area with grasses will create an environment for small world dinosaurs or animals. These could be in an area of a setting or even in large tyres. A stage made out of decking or wooden blocks with a few chairs in front will encourage children to sing and dance and maybe make up songs and dances.

Large shrubs, bamboo, or even planted pots with a variety of grasses or tall plants can make a magical and enclosed setting for all types of small world play, or a quiet space to chat with friends. Look critically at your outdoor space and see whether there are any areas that are underused or could be changed. If you are undertaking a large scale development project of your outdoor space it is important to involve the children. It is surprising what wonderful ideas they will come up with and hopefully you will be able to incorporate some of these into

Attractive shelters made for relatively little expense at Bus Stop Preschool

the final design. Choose plants that will provide items for children to collect and use in their play. Many plants have seedheads that can be used but it is important to ensure that they are suitable in gardens for children. There is a list of plants which should be avoided in Every Nursery Needs a Garden (Watts 2011) Chapter 3 or online at: https://www.rhs.org.uk/advice/profile?pid=524.

Small shelters can be made out of natural materials for relatively little cost and they can be adapted to meet the children's play needs as required. At Bus Stop nursery they have made good use of wooden pallets, some stout branches and netting to make different areas to encourage imaginative play.

Involve children in planting pots to create a jungle feel

Provision of materials

In woodland, it may be necessary to provide some string or rope, scissors or secateurs, trowels and magnifying glasses. A storage container on wheels provides safe storage and children will enjoy pulling it along with ropes attached to the front. By adding tools and resources that will be effective in the area you use, you will encourage the children to think about using the natural resources around them. For example scissors make great tools for cutting leaves and grasses, not just string.

Small paper bags for collecting things, trowels for digging, hammers and mallets need to be available. Additional resources such as water, paintbrushes and small jars are good if children have shown an interest in painting and mixing. Adults need to be creative and respond to the children's

Cutting leaves encourages coordination and concentration

ideas and interests. Hopefully they will be able to resources items to encourage and extend the ideas of the children.

Additional loose parts

Every setting needs to have some space dedicated to a collection of loose parts. The theory of loose parts was devised by Simon Nicholson in the 1970s and has had an impact on architects and designers as they design play spaces. It is however very easy to use his ideas in any setting.

Loose parts are materials that can be moved, carried, combined, designed and redesigned in a multitude of ways. In general we would advocate the inclusion of as many natural materials as possible. Children need to be supported in their play and this may include additional clearing up as parts get distributed in a variety of different places. Parts need to be stored so children can access them easily and know they can use them in whatever way they wish, then when they have finished they know where to return the loose parts. Adults will need to replenish and refresh the collections in order to sustain and develop play, and equally children can help here with collecting natural resources when they are out and about – sticks, acorns, fir cones and, more challenging, some logs if you are fortunate enough to have access to a newly felled tree.

**Collections of natural materials and other loose parts at
Randolph Beresford Nursery offer open access to a wide variety
of resources**

Evidence from Hyndman et al. (2014) demonstrates that playing with loose parts increases levels of creative and imaginative play and children play more co-operatively and socialise more. Loose parts also facilitate communication and negotiation skills when added to an outdoor play space (Maxwell et al. 2008).

Look at some of the ideas in the resource list and involve parents in helping to supply any items. Make a photographic display of items you need and put it where parents can see it as a regular reminder.

Children will begin to work in small groups as they plan their play. The provision of a length of hose or a small ladder may stimulate them to build a fire engine. So often the play will take its own course as children are able to construct, deconstruct and then construct again to develop their own ideas and imaginative thinking. Problem solving features highly as children look at the selection of items and work out how to use them to fit in with their ideas.

Detailed information in the provision and use of loose parts can be downloaded in a pdf file of the loose-parts-play toolkit published in Scotland from: www.hub.careinspectorate.com/media/405223/loose-parts-play-toolkit.pdf.

Suggested resource list as a starting point

- Small lengths of plastic and rubber hose
- Plastic guttering
- Small tyres
- Crates, pallets or boxes
- Baskets of different shapes and sizes
- Buckets and tubs of different sizes
- Large and small cardboard boxes
- Lengths of rope and string
- Pulleys
- Small wheelbarrows and trolleys
- Scoops, trowels and spoons of different sizes
- Logs, branches and twigs
- Collections of pebbles, shells, conkers, acorns, leaves, seedheads, bark, flower petals, feathers (children can often help to resource these collections themselves). Encourage parents to bring things in they might have collected on holiday or when outdoors with their children.
- Groundsheets, carpet squares, small cushions.

Visit charity shops, scrap yards and car boot sales. Involve parents, maybe having a visual display and photographs of some of the items you need. As the collection develops and more people become involved, there will be other exciting items that you can provide.

Developing imagination and curiosity through the Characteristics of Effective Learning

The Characteristics of Effective Learning (Early Education 2012) give three headings which are key to stimulating the beginnings of imaginative development: Playing and Exploring, Active Learning, and Creating and Thinking Critically (see below).

> *Children need to be able to find out and explore, play with what they know and be willing to have a go. They need to be involved and able to concentrate, to keep trying and enjoy achieving what they set out to do. To begin to operate creatively they need to be able to have their own ideas, to make links and choose ways to do things.*
>
> (https://www.foundationyears.org.uk/files/2012/07/Development-
> Matters-in-the-Early-Years-Foundation-Stage.pdf)

In this short observation we see how a child who is only 18 months old is able to do all of these things in a new environment.

W. (aged 18 months) was able to spend some time in a Forest School environment. She particularly enjoyed the mud kitchen and demonstrated a high level of concentration as she began to play imaginatively. She spent some time lifting and moving the pans around. She picked up a spoon and used it to make stirring movements in a large pan. She then put that pan down and chose an even bigger one which she had trouble lifting on her own and wanted to put it in a microwave oven which had been provided as part of the play kitchen. She asked her mother to open the door using the words 'door door' then put the pan inside with a little help, closed the door, pressed the knobs and made the sound of the 'beep beep' of a microwave.

First time in a mud kitchen – making choices and links

She was showing that she could make the link between the real and the pretend microwave oven. She explored independently and led her own play. She only asked for help when she couldn't do something herself and showed a high level of concentration and involvement throughout her play in this setting. Early pretend play has been seen to be associated with increased creative performance later (Russ 2004).

Promoting the characteristics of effective learning outdoors

Playing and exploring

Less verbal children may be able, through play, to demonstrate their needs and feelings, helping adults to clue in to their thinking. Play develops competencies that lead to increased confidence and resilience. Undirected play:

> *allows children to learn how to work in groups to share, to negotiate, to resolve conflicts and to learn self advocacy skills. When play is allowed to be child driven, children practice decision making skills, move at their own pace, discover their own areas of interest and ultimately engage fully in the passions they wish to pursue . . . when play is controlled by adults, children acquiesce to adult rules and concerns and lose some of the benefits play offers them, particularly in developing creativity, leadership and group skills.*
>
> (Ginsburg 2007, Para. 4 The benefits of play)

CASE STUDY: THE ROPE

Children at the Randolph Beresford Early Years Centre are encouraged to use their initiative and develop their own ideas. They come from a range of cultural and social backgrounds and for many English is an Additional Language. Staff do not pre-plan activities at Little Forest School other than maybe providing additional resources to extend a learning theme. They take their cue from the children and offer continuous support through observation and by asking appropriate questions.

At the beginning of a session children are encouraged to think what they would like to do before they set off. R decided he would like a rope and was encouraged to find the rope basket, and choose what he wanted. He chose a red rope. He was carrying an action man and looked at this as though he wanted to tie the rope around it. He then looked up at the roof of the cabin.

Ad. 'Do you have an idea?'

R. 'You get idea you need a rope.'

Ad. 'Can you tell me your plan?'

Ma. 'My plan is run and jump.'

R. 'Oh can we . . . up . . .', points to roof.

Ad. 'Do you want to get the man up there?'

R. nods yes, then Ma. picks up the other end of the rope. 'You hang it, you tie it and then just leave it.'

They pull it around laughing at each other. They start to run around pulling it. Other children join in and it becomes a great game for the group.

R. is still leading, holding his action man but Ma. is physically stronger and now moves the direction of the game until Y joins them.

Y. 'No this way, pull this way.'

They cooperate sufficiently to enable the game to last for around ten minutes, continuously moving together around the space.

The group are cooperating sufficiently to enable them to move successfully round a large area

(Ad. is adult. Children: R. Ma. N. Y.)

As it is still early in their school year, many of the children still operate independently, but this study shows the development of group interaction and social skills as the children worked and had fun together. It also shows how the adult facilitates and children are beginning to think about ideas and plans.

Adults need to think creatively about the outdoor space and how it can be used to encourage unstructured children's play. In an online review, 'Play Naturally' (Playday 2006), commissioned by the children's play council, there is strong reaffirmation of the essential nature of play in childhood development. Children prefer natural environments to play in as these help to develop all types of play. There is also evidence that a natural setting can reduce bullying. Vegetation and other natural features can create enclosed areas to help different groups play together with a wider range of activities, leading to better overall concentration and motor skills.

Karen Malone and Paul Tranter (2003) suggest that a play area that can be changed and modified provides more opportunities for environmental learning with corresponding behavioural consequences. Moore and Wong (1997) look at different aspects of play and how nature is important for children to develop properly through play. They assert that the type of place where children play has a direct influence on the quality of play.

Planning your outdoor space to include exploration spaces, wild flowers and plants which children are allowed to pick to use in their play, providing logs, branches, cones, shells and sand will all encourage rich exploratory play. (See chapter 3 of *Every Nursery Needs a Garden*, Watts 2011.)

Finding out and exploring

Being outdoors for as much time as possible will offer young children greater opportunities for exploration and discovery. From the moment they can crawl, babies will set off to see what they can find. Whilst we need to avoid objects such as small stones and pebbles, we need to offer them spaces with different textures and objects they can safely explore. Children will learn

Exploring snow.
So much fun!

from direct contact with natural elements and can show high levels of involvement as they explore sand, water, rain or snow.

If we enable them to interact with the elements in a safe but fun way they will develop in confidence and be able to discover more for themselves.

CASE STUDY: EXPLORING THE ENVIRONMENT

Mum was collecting M. from nursery with D. in the pushchair. They had to walk down a woodland track which had several large puddles and was surrounded by several large trees, which offered a beautiful dappled sunlight.

Mum was not in any hurry and took D. out of the pushchair and allowed both children time to explore the puddles. M. collected fallen leaves and petals, which she placed on a large piece of silver birch bark and then floated it in the puddle. She moved her 'boat' very gently with a large stick that she had found.

D. enjoyed walking in the puddle. The movement of the water fascinated him when he moved; he would toddle forwards and around and watch the flow of the water in the sunlight. He stumbled a little, lost his balance and promptly sat down in the middle of the puddle. Instead of removing him, mum allowed him to stay there. He began to splash the water with his hands and giggled in sheer delight! This attracted M.'s attention and she too sat down in her puddle – both children giggling with pure pleasure.

The practitioner, who had been chatting with the mum, commented on the wonderful learning experiences for the children. Mum's response was 'We can always have a wash and clean later, we're in no hurry today'.

Play continued for a further 10 minutes, and only came to an end when the older child asked what lunch would be. Mum replied 'Macaroni cheese', and both quickly got up ready to leave.

(Child M. 4 years old and Child D. 2 years old)

This observation shows the importance of allowing time for children to explore in their own way and at their own pace. The environment with the puddles and bright sunlight gave new opportunities for exploration and learning. The woodland setting also offered a relaxing environment for both the children and the parent. Helen Bilton mentions that if children are given time for uninterrupted play, allowing their thoughts and ideas to develop, they become more motivated to learn (Bilton 2010).

The actions of the parent in this case study enabled both children to fully explore in the way they wished. If she had intervened and removed the younger child when he sat down, there could have been a very different scenario with tears and frustrations for everyone.

The children were both dressed in appropriate clothing and Mum was sufficiently relaxed to allow them time to explore in the way they wished and finish their play as they felt ready.

Using what they know in their play

Older children need access to a variety of resources outdoors to encourage them to play at a deeper level and develop their imaginations. Small hidey holes for babies will become the starting point for the sophisticated shelters designed and built by four and five year olds. Play involves doing, exploring, discovering, failing and succeeding. Children create and then recreate their own worlds using the knowledge gained from previous play.

(Watts 2013, p. 13)

Close observation of young children reveals the many links that appear in their play as they build on their first-hand memories and experiences to extend and develop their own play.

Being willing to have a go

Outdoor spaces offer endless opportunities to encourage safe risk taking and offer new experiences. A tree trunk is there to be climbed, log stepping stones are for jumping, while a small wildlife

CASE STUDY: LIGHTING THE FIRE

At the Bus Stop nursery, children regularly watch an adult light a fire. They learn the basic safety rules and walk round the back of the circle to take their places around the fire. They learn about safe places to make the fire. During a free play session where children just play in the woodland space, one child recreated this experience. He carefully selected a spot and built a pretend fire out of small sticks and leaves. He then placed a large log at the edge to mark out a fireplace. He picked up two sticks which became his imaginary matches. He carefully leant over the log and pretended to light his fire. He remained in position looking at the pretend fire until he was called away as the play session ended.

Lighting the fire: using what he knows in his imaginary play

pond waits to be explored. In an urban setting, pallets and planks offer opportunities for physical challenge and it is easy to provide spaces for children to plant and grow flowers and vegetables.

Planks, pallets and logs provide challenging opportunities for children's movement skills

Active learning

As children explore the natural world around them they will find small creatures, observe plants, trees and birds. They will become aware of the seasons and how to plant and care for their own crops. With appropriate adult support, they will acquire new knowledge and use this to inform their decision making. Hopefully this will be sustained through their adult life as they contribute towards sustainability. Sensitive intervention can encourage and deepen learning itself but also encourages the child to regard learning as an exciting journey.

CASE STUDY: FISHING

A large muddy puddle at Randolph Beresford Early Years Centre prompted the idea of fishing and the practitioner made herself a fishing rod with a stick and some string. Y. wanted a fishing rod and was encouraged to find a suitable stick and go to the resource centre to find some string.

Because the adult was fishing too, the play was sustained over a long period of time. Imaginary fish were being caught and escaping.

Y. 'We need a bucket.'

He ran off to find one. 'They go in there – they not like it – they still jumping out.'

He bends down to the puddle to get water in the bucket.

'They still jumping – need more water.'

As children wanted to join in the adult asked what they would need to make their fishing lines. They were encouraged to go off to find appropriate resources and needed help only with tying the string to the rope. Play was extended too as the adult sang an impromptu song and encouraged the children to make up verses as well as singing '12345 once I caught a fish alive'.

Having an adult joining in extends concentration and makes it all so much more fun

Being involved and concentrating

An outdoor environment may help children to concentrate on their play as there is often less noise and distraction than in the indoor classroom setting. Children respond naturally to the outdoor environment and as play develops a sensitive adult will ensure that there are additional resources to extend it. A muddy puddle and a stick will enable a lively toddler to become deeply involved and totally absorbed in this world. Older children, too, become absorbed in their play with natural elements of sand, mud and water.

Research by Ferre Laevers et al. (2005) links this ability of young children to become deeply involved in an activity with increased levels of self-esteem and a state of wellbeing. Dr William Bird (2007) outlined research which suggested that children diagnosed with ADHD will benefit from more time spent outdoors and in green spaces. The research asserted that children are far more able to concentrate, to focus and pay attention after being outside. The authors suggested that all children's attentional functioning could benefit from incorporating vegetation into places where children live and play. Keep this in mind as you plan your outdoor space; the benefits of being surrounded by plants and trees cannot be over-estimated.

Keeping on trying

Watching a baby trying to crawl and reach for something just out of reach demonstrates that this characteristic is present from a very early age. If adults offer positive support and encouragement, children will learn to overcome the difficulties of walking through long grass or avoiding brambles and set themselves challenges as they climb trees or build dens.

Connie was so proud of her physical achievement in being able to crawl to the end of the tree trunk and jump off on her own, that she kept repeating the activity and did not want to stop. This aspect of learning reaches out across the curriculum. It may mean creating an art work from natural materials. It could be setting up a water system either in sand or mud or using tubes and gutters and watching the first trickle.

CASE STUDY: CONNIE

Connie (age 3.5) was the only child in a small group who found it difficult to crawl along a fallen tree trunk without help. She was not confident and initially needed quite a lot of adult support, both physical and emotional. Each time she did this she gained slowly in confidence and would go back to try again. After five attempts with adult help, she was confident enough to try on her own and showed immense pleasure when she jumped off without help. She kept doing this and later that morning was observed climbing unaided to the top of an A frame ladder leaning against a tree.

Enjoying achieving what she has set out to do

Creating and thinking critically

Having their own ideas

Children need to find their own challenges and then use their critical thinking skills to set their boundaries and targets. Rule making, codes and passwords become an important part of the sophisticated play of older children. This has its basis in the play systems established in the early years.

> A group of six children were playing outdoors in an environment that offered a tree house and plenty of wild open space. Children's ages ranged from five to 13. Observation showed that the older children invented the rules and varied them as the game progressed, to meet the social and play needs of the younger children. There was a competitive element with teams chasing and hunting down the other side but again the older children ensured the younger ones played safely and were able to join in.

Children will have their own ideas and if offered suitable materials can create their own designs and patterns. Establish rich play opportunities with the provision of basic materials of sand, mud and water and talk and listen to children as they play. Providing a range of natural materials such as flower petals, bark and leaves, encourages additional creativity and allows children the freedom to discover the rules of pattern making and design. At a Forest School session, a child had made a square shape on the ground and was getting the other children to aim their sticks into the box from his 'throwing line'. His game included several rules at the start, mainly about who would go first and how many sticks they can have, but once the game got going, others would think of new rules.

Making links

Children benefit from an environment where they can control the space, explore and experiment, destroy and rebuild. Outdoors, they can influence their surroundings and also begin to take responsibility for them. They need space for 'being' as well as 'doing'.

Offer resources which will help them build their own spaces and encourage their problem solving skills. It is possible to create a den even on a hard safety surface. Ideas for this are offered in the chapter on building structures. If the den needs to be packed away each day, the children will become more adept each day at setting it up.

A journey stick can be made to reflect a walk the children have been on. They collect items of special interest and meaning as they go and using rubber bands attach them to the stick. This then reminds them of the journey they have been on and encourages them to use their imagination to make links and recreate the journey in their mind.

Making a journey stick

Choosing ways to do things

Careful observation will show how well children can plan their own activity and whether they are able to adapt if things are not going so well. Can they suggest a different strategy and are they able to review how well their approach has worked? It is important to observe whether children can make predictions and test out their own ideas. Children may need initial adult support to encourage them to think and talk about how they reach conclusions and solve problems.

CASE STUDY: FROM RANDOLPH BERESFORD EARLY YEARS CENTRE

Children enjoyed splashing through muddy puddles and balancing on a variety of planks.

Av. showed increasing confidence as she climbed up a narrow plank onto a large cable drum. At the top she needed some adult help to get down. M. joined in this game too.

A. to M. 'How could you get down without my help? What could you do so you could get down by yourselves?'

M. ran off and returned with a short plank. She held it against the cable drum and after a while seemed to realise it was too short (unfit for purpose). She went back to the woodstore and returned carrying a longer plank helped by the adult. She placed it just on the edge of the drum. Av. tentatively placed a foot on it and realised it was unsafe. M. looked at it and despite A. asking how she could make it safe found it difficult to understand how to move it further up onto the drum to make it safer. Adult and child worked together until eventually they reached a satisfactory and safe outcome and Av. was able to descend. 'Wibble wobble' she said as she carefully climbed down. She returned to complete the circuit several more times with ever increasing confidence.

Having a supportive adult to ask questions, encourage and suggest when necessary enables a high level of problem solving in young children

(A. is adult, Av. and M. two children)

Conclusion

The importance of taking children outside everyday cannot be stressed too much. It is good for their physical health and general development as well as offering an exciting space for them to enjoy and explore. Through exploration they will be constantly learning new things as they interact with each other and the world around them. Adults who share these experiences will also gain satisfaction and enjoyment as they watch the children make progress and also as they in turn develop their own imagination, finding ways to enhance the learning opportunities for the children. Adults need to be creative about the ways they utilise the available spaces in different ways to offer a wide range of exciting opportunities: places to run, jump, climb and explore, but also places to be quiet, to spend time observing the wildlife around, and places where children can experiment with a range of messy materials, construct and move parts around in a variety of ways.

Imagination develops in the first five years of life and children need to be able to explore and develop their own ideas. They need the time and the spaces but they also need adults whom they trust and with whom they can share their ideas. Adults will need to observe and respond to the children's ideas providing resources in response to these in order to extend the children's interests and knowledge.

POINTS FOR DISCUSSION

- If you are involved with babies, are they given daily opportunities to be outside and explore a variety of resources?

- Are you able to develop a collection of loose parts? Can you provide a special place for storage? Discuss how you work together with children to keep it tidy and well stocked

- Think about the quality and variety of resources you have for imaginative play. Do children have easy access to open ended resources?

- Are all practitioners in your setting familiar with the Leuven involvement scales? Are they able to apply them in practice?

- Are practitioners aware of how to use provocations to extend children's imaginative thinking?

USEFUL RESOURCES

Loose Parts: Inspiring Play in Young Children by Lisa Daly (Red Leaf Press 2014)

Loose Parts 2 Inspiring Play with Infants and Toddlers by Miriam Meloglovsky (Red Leaf Press 2016) – These two books are well illustrated with lots of good ideas and cover the element of safety as well as child development.

Stanley's Stick by John Hegley (Hodder Children's Books 2012) – A lovely story showing how a stick can be just about anything.

Useful website: www.psychologytoday.com. 'The need for pretend play' in *Psychology Today*. https://www.psychologytoday.com/blog/beautiful-minds/201203/the-need-pretend-play-in-child-development

Bibliography

Bilton, H. (2010) *Outdoor Learning in the Early Years*. London: Routledge.

Bird, W. (2007) *Natural Thinking: Investigating the Links between the Natural Environment, Biodiversity and Mental Health*. Sandy, Bedfordshire: RSPB.

Early Education (2012) *Development Matters in the Early Years Foundation Stage (EYFS)*. Available at: https://www.foundationyears.org.uk/files/2012/07/Development-Matters-in-the-Early-Years-Foundation-Stage.pdf.

Einstein, A. (1955) 'Old man's advice to youth: Never lose a holy curiosity', *LIFE magazine*, 2 May: 64.

Froebel, F. (1887) *The Education of Man*, translated by W. Hailmann. New York, London: D. Appleton Century.

Gibson, J. (1986) *The Ecological Approach to Visual Perception*. London: Psychology Press.

Ginsberg, K.R. (2007) 'The importance of play in promoting healthy child development and maintaining strong parent–child bonds', *Paediatrics* 119(1), also online at http://pediatrics.aappublications.org/content/119/1/182.

Hughes, F.P. (2010) *Children, Play and Development*. London: Sage Publications.

Hughes, J. (1910) *Froebel's Educational Laws for All Teachers 1897*. New York: D. Appleton and Company.

Hyndman, B., Benson, A., Ullah, S. and Telford, A. (2014) 'Evaluating the effects of the Lunchtime Enjoyment Activity and Play (LEAP) school playground intervention on children's quality of life, enjoyment and participation in physical activity', *BMC Public Health* 14(1): 164.

Laevers, F., Daems, M., De Bruckyere, G., Declerq, B., Moons, J., Silkens, K., Snoeck, G. and Van Kesse, M. (2005) *Well-being and Involvement in Care: A Process Orientated Self Evaluation Instrument for Care Settings*. Leuven University, Belgium. Available online at https://www.kindengezin.be/img/sics-ziko-manual.pdf.

Malone, K. and Tranter, P. (2003) 'Children's environmental learning and the use, design and management of school grounds', *Children, Youth and Environments* 13(2): 283–303.

Maxwell, L.E., Mitchell, M.N. and Evans, G. (2008) 'Effects of play equipment and loose parts on preschool children's outdoor play behaviour: An observational study and design intervention', *Children, Youth and Environments* 18(2): 36–63.

Moore, R. and Wong, H. (1997) *Natural Learning*. Berkeley: MIG Communications.

Playday (2006) 'Play naturally'. Available at: www.playday.org.uk/campaigns-3/previous-campaings/2006-play-naturally/

Russ, S.W. (2004) *Play in Child Development and Psychotherapy*. Mahwah NJ: Erlbaum.

Watts, A.C. (2011) *Every Nursery Needs a Garden*. London: Routledge.

3 The Forest School background

The growing popularity of Forest School in the UK has meant we are now seeing more practitioners being introduced to the Forest School ethos in early years settings and primary and secondary schools.

In this chapter, we will look at:

■ the Forest School ethos and how it is increasing in popularity

■ different types of Forest School practice within the early years, the levels to which they cover the Forest School principles and the long-term sustainability

■ the benefits of long-term Forest School sessions with fully trained practitioners in appropriate environments to enable creativity

■ safety awareness and ideas to try for Forest School activities

■ options for settings with no links to wider outdoor spaces.

The Forest School ethos

This has been developed over the past few years since the early experiences seen in the Danish and European settings, where children would spend large parts of their day outdoors using natural resources in all weathers. When Forest School came over to the UK in the 1990s it was initially provided by a few early years settings. This has been well documented by Sara Knight (one of the Directors of the Forest School Association) in her books on Forest School (Knight 2009 and Knight 2013). Over time, research has found that the more variety of outdoor learning approaches children experience, the greater the diversity and learning potential there is for the child. As the benefits of being outdoors are now known to help with problems of behaviour and mental health, Forest Schools are being seen as a possible answer to improving the well-being of children, young people and even adults. With all these trends in mind, we need to explore the difference between what is Forest School and what could be classed as Outdoor Education.

The increased interest in Forest School (FS) led to the creation of the Forest School Association (FSA) in 2011, to ensure that the ethos and quality of Forest School practice and quality of training for new practitioners are maintained. During this first gathering, where over 100 practitioners from around the UK participated, six guiding principles for the Forest School Ethos were tabled and agreed. More detailed information can be found on the FSA website; a brief outline of the principles is given below.

These are:

1. FS is a long-term process of regular sessions, rather than one-off or infrequent visits; the cycle of planning, observation, adaptation and review links each session.

2. FS takes place in a woodland or natural environment to support the development of a relationship between the learner and the natural world.

3. FS uses a range of learner-centred processes to create a community for being, development and learning.

4. FS aims to promote the holistic development of all those involved, fostering resilient, confident, independent and creative learners.

5. FS offers learners the opportunity to take supported risks appropriate to the environment and to themselves.

6. FS is run by qualified Forest School practitioners who continuously maintain and develop their professional practice

The Forest School Association website highlights these principles and ethos as well as giving information on where to find trained practitioners and providers for training. It also explains the history of the 'Forest school trainers network GB' and the history behind the three levels of recognised qualifications, which were accepted by OFQUAL (February 2013), and published on the English Qualification Credit Framework (QCF) (March 2013), which has undergone a review (2017). The FSA website has more information on this, plus research material, good practice and links to local FSA groups (see useful resources below).

Forest School is predominantly child-led and run over a long period of time and where possible in a woodland area. It is this regular and long-term exposure to the outdoor environment where the child can experience all seasons of the year which enables the most valuable outcomes for their deeper level of learning and wellbeing.

Types of Forest Schools

There are many established early years settings and primary schools who have trained practitioners as part of their team or who bring in freelance practitioners to deliver a programme of Forest School. The levels of delivery vary. Some embrace the full Forest School ethos, are based in woodland with no building structures and children experience all seasons. Others take groups out to a nearby location where walking to the site is of equal importance to being in the woodland. Some may have the use of minibuses to take them further afield. Some make use of their local parks, or areas of the school grounds that have been adapted to take small groups. This may mean that children experience blocks of Forest School sessions, which are still of importance, but could not be classed as long-term involvement.

The benefits of embracing the long-term Forest School ethos have been seen to support children's development in their physical abilities, ability to take and manage risks, improved stamina and resilience, knowledge and caring of the natural world, social and emotional development, language and communication, and finally their ability to be imaginative and creative within the woodland environment.

Trained Forest School Practitioners will have particular skills that they want the child to experience over time and this may take place as planned for a particular session, but a good practitioner will take the lead from the child's interests. Quite often weather, the environment or an experience that the child has just had will offer a new interest on that day and a new learning pathway will be taken.

Some qualities for a good Forest School Practitioner prior to training might include:

- having an understanding of child behaviour and development

- having a love for the outdoor environment in all weathers – so always looking on the bright side!

- understanding children's learning styles

- understanding basic flora and fauna – this can be expanded as you develop your practice

- understanding the wildlife that visits your area – know your basics and learn with the children as you develop your practice with the many resources available.

If you decide to do a Forest School Practitioner training course either at Level 2 or Level 3 (a source of training providers can be found on the FSA website), you will learn the FSA ethos and some of the following (the first two items are pre-course requirements):

- hold a 16 hours outdoor first aid certificate (with paediatric extension section to be included)

- hold a current DBS and have an understanding of child safety and safeguarding procedures

- training in tool use – initial use following your Forest School training and then should be ongoing CPD. This can be found via the many FSA cluster groups or Forest School training providers

- training in fire use – initial use following your training and then should be ongoing CPD

- training in woodland sustainability – understand your site's care and management programme – this should be a continuous programme built into your site and working with the land owner, from whom you should have written permission to undertake your Forest School activities

- training in risk management – policies/risk assessment/looking at your site – again this should be continuous as you develop your practice. In the beginning, practitioners tend to be over-cautious; as they become confident, so too does their practice and reflection of the experiences they offer.

Once trained, it is good practice to refresh and maintain your initial skills and also try:

- finding ideas – activities, games, experiences

- improving your observation skills – knowing when to interact and knowing when to observe the children

- meeting up with other trained practitioners at the many CPD trainings or FSA cluster gathering.

When planning a session, practitioners do not always need a planned 'craft activity'. The Forest School ethos of child-led learning might be that not every child's interest will follow this 'activity' path. If the child, for example, has been involved in mixing potions for most of the session, then observe what they are doing. Are they using all the materials that your environment offers? Is there anything that you could add to support them? Could a new natural material be added – dried petals from a floral bouquet? Or could a new piece of equipment be found – a giant spoon for example? Perhaps the discovery of a recipe card, shown in pictures with the ingredients found around the environment with a small basket for collecting them, could encourage a new lead or story? What scale is their potion-making? Is it with small bottles or old coconut shells? Could it be decreased or increased in size for say a 'dragon or a unicorn'?

Practitioners gather for a variety of skills training, sharing and learning new ideas

The introduction of bigger tools offers a new line of learning for their play, and will provide new resources for physical development

During a particular session, adults had planned for the children to use the bow saw and make wood cookies. However during the night it rained heavily, which produced very large puddles. The children were so involved with the water that their stories of boats, fishing rods and pirate ships were followed instead.

The ethos of Forest School clearly allows for the child to be an independent learner who will learn to take and manage their own risks by being exposed to new, stimulating environments over a period of time. We can see this happening with many Forest School experiences, and in Chapter 1 we referred to Bill Maxwell's paper (Education Scotland 2013), as he highlighted three recurring themes, which were: the need to help children take greater responsibility for planning their own learning; the need to establish open-ended approaches to learning which is the 'What if?' or 'What happens if?', as suggested by Anna Craft (2002); and then the need to use external partnerships and stimuli to broaden and enhance the learning experience.

Types of Forest School practice

As practitioners, we need to reflect upon the way the Forest School ethos can be used in all settings, whether this is the full ethos or parts of it, in order to enrich the imagination and the learning of our children. Children need the outdoors to stimulate all of their creativity. Practitioners need to think creatively on how to use what they have. Doireann O'Connor, in her paper 'Creativity in childhood: The role of education', states, 'Educators who rise to the creativity challenge will be well rewarded in rich teaching experiences and the joy of seeing children reach their creative potential in supportive and integrated learning systems' (O'Connor 2012).

We have mentioned what the ideal Forest School approach should be, but the reality of this is not always possible. What is important is the experience the children are gaining. Being in an outdoor environment, whatever its size or facilities, is better than nothing at all. Often over time, practice, experiences and the environment can all be enhanced to come closer to the ideal Forest School ethos.

A number of urban early years settings, who do not have access to a large woodland or open space, have been creative within their own outdoor areas, by introducing 'wildness' to their settings. Logs of different shapes and sizes, planting of trees or large bushes, bamboo and long flowing grasses in pots will create a jungle like atmosphere. Digging up the concrete or paving slabs and replacing them with soil, rocks or boulders also gives a child that wild and free experience. Introducing wildlife areas for butterflies, creating bug houses or just keeping a pile of logs to encourage insects to make their home, will all add to the richness of the child's learning, understanding and wellbeing.

Once a tarmac playground this area now offers a more natural environment for children to explore and investigate

Creative resourcing is vital in these circumstances and the careful consideration of rotation of these resources throughout the year will offer children new learning opportunities, as well as ensuring some sustainability for the actual site that you use. Forest School practitioners who use a woodland or open area also need to monitor their use of the site. We must reflect upon the ecological impact and sustainability of the sites used and how the constant footfall and use can be managed. You may be fortunate to have a couple of areas within the site that will allow you to rotate the Forest School programme, in order for the site to renew its growth, allowing nature to return; or you may be creative with the areas you have and rotate the activities, allowing the more popular one time to 'heal'. However you decide to manage your site, careful creativity is key to a sustainable site.

Since the formation of the FSA, several regions have formed cluster groups to enable all trained practitioners and those undertaking their Level 3 or Level 2 qualifications to meet up so they can learn new skills, share ideas and good practice. Practitioners need to consider, as we have mentioned before, how they work with their children outdoors. Are they wanting to follow the Forest School ethos following the six principles as described above, or are they more akin to linking to an Outdoor Education, Bushcraft, environmental work or a nature nursery programme? Whatever you decide, just getting children outside is crucial to their long-term development, mental wellbeing and appreciation of the natural environment.

Now we look at some creative Forest School ideas for practitioners to use within their setting. We need to give consideration to safety for both the practitioner and children.

Forest School – games to keep you safe

In Forest School, children are taught a number of skills to keep them safe and develop a code of behaviour. Using a whistle for the 'Stop and come to me' is a very effective method when the FS practitioner needs the children to come immediately. Different games can be played, first when the children are in sight and then when the leader is not quite in full view.

A particular favourite with all children is '123 where are you'. This is a 'hide and seek' type game, but the difference is that you want to be found. The game is used to give the children a method, so that if they find themselves out of sight of an adult or are unsure of their surroundings, they can call this message out, and they will always get a reply of '123 here we are'. At first when playing this game with early years, the children will stay close with the adult, gradually over time, some will want to find their own places to hide and have the confidence to call out independently. You will need to consider this approach and include it in your risk assessment for the areas you use and the children you have. In the beginning, children often run too quickly in the direction they first hear the call. It is the role of the practitioner to get them to slow down and make regular calls so they can really listen to the direction the calls are calling from. This listening skill is also teaching children to use their peripheral listening skills. One parent from a local setting explained how at the airport their child lost contact with them for a few moments, but instantly shouted out '123 where are you', the parents heard her and knew the response she would be waiting for and they were able to find each other.

Some safety games for Forest School

Keeping safe – boundaries of play and risk

Where the outdoor area is a much larger space, 'boundary' ties are often used. One setting uses blue rope tied around certain trees or features, to indicate where the children can go up to but not beyond. The practitioner will explain if there is a particular danger that needs to be highlighted and the children will 'walk' the boundary during their first few sessions to see where there could be a risk. Some settings get the children to take turns to do the 'Safety Talk' prior to starting their session; this helps them remember the boundary area and any other safety items you may use. Again, repetition is key.

It is a good thing to also allow the children to identify where they think there could be a risk and allow them to mark it in the same way as the setting has chosen. For example, another setting has a large pond on their site, which dries up during the year. The children mark this area with stick flags on the bank when the water is present and where the water is the deepest. The children experience and understand the cause and effect that rain has on the area and therefore have a better understanding of the dangers.

Keeping safe – fire and tools

Forest School Practitioners trained to Level 3 may have a fire either in a purpose-made fire bowl or direct on the ground within a fire pit area. Many adults are often nervous at the thought of introducing fire in a space with very young children.

However, the risk benefits far outweigh the negative risks, and careful preparation of the children beforehand will ensure their safety. The sights, sounds and colour of flames fascinate children and we will talk more about how fire can be used in a creative way later in this book.

Portable fire bowls can be used where the ground is unsuitable for direct fires due to the possible spread of underground heat

Fires built on the ground do not need to be large

Large fire circles are needed for large group cooking, where you require different cooking areas for heat levels.

Playing simple games to encourage correct movement and behaviour around the fire circle, before a real fire is introduced, will aid children's knowledge and understanding. It will also alleviate any emotional fears that a child may have. A simple swapping game, calling two children's names for them to swap seats/area, is often a fun approach, or the children can use some head-dresses and take on an animal role and swap with their matching pairs. The practitioners need to reinforce the message of praise when they move around the outside of the circle and not through the circle. Another setting gets the children to shout out 'Elephant' if anyone walks inside the fire circle, and reinforces the message that 'an elephant never forgets to walk outside the fire circle'.

CASE STUDY: USING A FIRE STEEL

During an after-school Forest School, two children were given opportunities to use a fire steel to light a fire. T. (age 7) had been practising this skill for some time, the younger child (O.) (age 4) who had only been coming to the club for a few weeks, wanted to have a go at the fire lighting.

While T. was persevering with trying to light the cotton wool on the fire, O. was given a striker and with adult support (A.) was shown how to use it.

O. – 'it's not sparky' (when trying to use his fire steel).

The adult again supported him, showing him which parts needed to touch and how much pressure he needed to use.

O. – 'Why won't it go?' He keeps trying.

A. – 'It takes a lot of practice, keep going that's right, keep going.'

A. leaves O. to practise with another adult nearby, while she attends to T., who having lit the main campfire, now wants to make his own little fire. The adult gives him a large shell and some tinder and wool for him to use.

Meanwhile, the younger child is still persevering with support of the new adult. He eventually creates a very small spark.

O. – 'Ooo, look.'

Adult – 'That's it, keep going you've now made a baby spark, see if you can make a bigger one.'

He again keeps trying, but sees that the older boy is now lighting his own fire.

O. – 'Can I do one? It got a sparky' (talking to the leader who's now nearer to him).

A. – 'Yes you can, come around the fire circle and we will find you your own fire space.'

Smiling, he goes around with his striker and is given his own pile of cotton wool for him to have a go at lighting it.

Older child using steel perseveres to light the main fire for the group

. . . younger child with support has his first go at using a fire steel

Child is then given time to practise this new skill, with an adult close by for support when needed

Although O. did not finish the final task, his confidence level was very high following his disappointment at the start. Being allowed time to practise his skill without interference, but with support from the adults, he was able to gain small steps of achievement. His perseverance of the task lasted for nearly half an hour and then during other sessions and at home he was able to use this experience in his pretend play.

It should be mentioned that a fire does not need to be very large, it is not just for marshmallows, but can offer a whole range of experiences to an early years child. With fire and food, areas for hand washing need to be considered.

Hand washing ideas: using a large milk container cut in two, one child pours the water for the other to wash his hands

Creative fire and tool use

- Cooking either on a stick, in a foil bag, in a pan, a Dutch oven or in a paper bag; examples and recipes can be found on many websites or Pinterest

- Fire for warmth and comfort

- Pewter melting – see Chapter 7

- Charcoal – see Chapter 7

- Magical storytelling – fire dust – see Chapter 4.

The Forest School session may also include using a number of tools to support children's learning. The use and safety of these tools needs to be explained to the child and introduced gradually. Below are some of the tools used with examples of items that can be produced. It should be noted that using a tool does not have to result in an end product; sometimes just using it will satisfy a child.

■ Use of bow saw:

- wood cookies

- drum sticks

- stick feathers/candles

- firewood

■ Use of bill hook:

- splitting wood

- candle holders

- making musical instruments

■ Use of drills (from palm to rotary and auger bits):

- candle holders

- mice

- stick feathers/candles/threading disks

■ Use of knife:

- whittle end for cooking your marshmallow

- mice/people

- flowers

- feather sticks to enable fire lighting.

Feather sticks

Stick doll

Using bow saw

Games

Games are often used within Forest School for a number of reasons, learning a particular skill, socialising, keeping warm or just for fun. Equally children can invent their own games with rules, as mentioned in Chapter 2.

Some tried and tested games:

Finding worms/caterpillars

- Hidden worms (i.e. small coloured pieces of wool hidden on branches or bushes)
  - Children use their observation skills
  - Extension ideas – hide them much higher OR
  - Use pipe cleaners twisted higher – to allow for teamwork

- Kim's game
  - Hide objects along a small route; or on a log on the ground for the children to then try and remember OR
  - One group positions themselves along a short trail, the other group walks the trail to try and remember who they saw; an extension could be in what order they saw them.

- Is it natural or manmade?
  - Hide picture cards of wildlife and manmade objects on trees/branches
  - Sort them into who lives in the environment/who or what does not live here
  - Encourages care for the environment.

- Head bands – 'who am I?'
  - Have a selection of pictures for children to describe/guess the animal or bird OR
  - Can be played in teams – one team has the animal or bird pictures, the other team has the 'call' and must find their partner

- Mammoth, hunter, mouse
  - Game for two teams – similar to the hand game of 'scissors rock paper' with action poses
  - Whole team decides what they are and upon the count of three makes the action
  - The dominant character then chases the other team to catch them
  - Those who are caught become a member to their team Game continues until one team is out
  - Running to keep warm

**Finding clues –
what lives in the
woods**

■ Go fetch

- This could relate to a small list of leaf shapes or natural items,
- Can be done individually, in pairs or in teams
- Keeping warm.

Conclusion

The Forest School approach is about creating long-term 'emotional memories' in the early years, and offering a range of outdoor experiences throughout the year. This prepares children so they can draw upon these experiences later on in their school and possibly adult life. How you embrace the Forest School ethos and how you use your environment to get children outside will depend upon your area and facilities. What is evident is the value of offering enriched outdoor experiences.

Children need to have these hands-on experiences such as squelching in mud, or learning to use a testing stick before wading through big puddles. If they don't, they will soon learn the cause and effect of what happens to their boots! Practitioners and children will share the excitement of finding a worm or minibeast in the undergrowth, feel the wind and rain on their faces and learn together to recognise the sights and sounds of the natural world.

Good training is key for practitioners to deliver quality Forest School sessions. Continued professional development is needed to gain confidence and learn new skills and ideas from like-minded practitioners. Finally, knowing when to interact with the children and when to step back and let their play gain momentum naturally is equally important for the child's learning.

PRACTITIONERS' SAFETY POINTS

■ Do you have policies and risk assessments in place for tool work and fire?

■ Do your policies consider ratios when at Forest School or outside your normal grounds?

■ Consider the space you have for running games, and be aware of hazards.

■ When using fire ensure you have all the appropriate safety equipment, including a burns kit.

POINTS FOR DISCUSSION

■ What type of outdoor learning experience do you feel you offer?

■ How might you use your outdoor space to ensure sustainability?

■ What CPD training is available near you and can you access a FSA cluster group?

USEFUL RESOURCES/WEBSITES/BOOKS

■ Hammocks

■ Fabrics

■ Rope in a variety of lengths and thicknesses for swings or play

■ Straplines (webbing for tightrope walking/balance)

■ Ladders – can be rope or made with coppiced wood

■ Small tools – child access: spoons, trowels, hand rakes, hammers, mallets

■ Small tools – used under supervision: saws, billhooks, knives, drills

■ Buckets

■ Small logs and tree stumps

■ Cable drums

■ Guttering or tubes

- Collecting bags of various sizes

- Trollies for transporting kit

- Children's rucksacks – they can then take responsibility for some equipment

- Adult rucksack

- Hardwearing bowls and mugs for snacks.

Websites

Teacher Tom – blog – http://teachertomsblog.blogspot.co.uk/

Juliet Robinson – I'm a teacher get me outdoors – http://creativestarlearning.co.uk/

Forest School Association – www.forestschoolassociation

Learning outside the classroom – http://www.lotc.org.uk

Muddyfaces for FS resources – http://www.muddyfaces.co.uk

Books

International Perspectives on Forest School – Natural Spaces to Play and Learn by S. Knight (Sage 2013)

Risk and Adventure in Early Years Outdoor Play – Learning from Forest Schools by S. Knight (Sage 2011)

Make it Wild by J. Schofield and F. Danks (Frances Lincoln Ltd 2010)

Understanding the Danish Forest School Approach, Early Years in Practice by Jane Williams-Siegfredsen (Routledge 2012)

Bringing the Forest School Approach to your Early Years Practice by Karen Constable (Routledge 2014)

The Outdoor Classroom in Practice, Ages 3–7: A Month-by-Month Guide to Forest School Provision by Karen Constable (Routledge 2015)

'According to science, "Forest Bathing" has proven health benefits' by Natalie Olsen, and Juli Fraga, https://www.healthline.com/health/stress/forest-bathing-shinrin-yoku (5 June 2017)

Bibliography

Craft, A. (2002) *Creativity and Early Years Education.* London: Continuum Books.

Education Scotland (2013) *Creativity across Learning 3–18.* Available at: https://education.gov.scot/improvement/Documents/Creativity/CRE1_WhatAreCreativitySkills/Creativity3to18.pdf.

Knight, S. (2009) *Forest Schools and Outdoor Learning in the Early Years.* London: Sage.

Knight, S. (2013) *Forest Schools and Outdoor Learning in the Early Years,* 2nd edition. London: Sage.

O'Connor, D. (2010) 'Creativity in childhood: The role of education', http://researchonline.nd.edu.au/cgi/viewcontent.cgi?article=1078&context=edu_conference

4 Communication in the natural world

Listening and speaking

The natural world offers endless opportunities for children to engage in conversation, whether it be for socialising, questioning or learning. Language is needed to solve problems, such as how to get their long branch through small gaps. Language is needed to express excitement as children discover conkers for the first time or spot a robin.

Here we will look at:

■ how children's listening and attention skills can be supported

■ how language might be enhanced in the natural environment

■ how children are given time to speak and be listened to

■ how vocabulary, imaginative and thinking language can flourish and be extended.

Development background to listening and attention

There is often a cacophony of sounds in an early years setting: children's chatter and laughter, adults, occasional recorded background music and even the resources in the setting; all have an impact and can sometimes interfere with the harmony of the environment.

Likewise, children's home environments are often filled with constant background sounds from radios, television and other recorded devices. This, together with the added increased use of screen time from digital devices, could be a possible factor for a number of attention and listening skills deficits that young children can display.

As children develop they will go through a series of attention levels. Psychologist Joan Reynell, in the 1970s, first defined these. The levels are broken down from birth through to when a child is of school age. By understanding these areas of child development practitioners are able to support children.

These levels are:

- **Distractibility**, 0–1 year: babies can only hold their attention for a few moments and they are easily distracted by new sounds or objects.

- **Single channel attention**, 1–2 years: children begin to focus their attention on one activity and do not like a spoken or visual distraction. We have all spoken to a child so engrossed in an activity that they appear not to hear us at all.

- **Single channel attention with more flexibility**, 2–3 years: children continue to focus on one activity and still find it difficult to shift their attention when spoken to. However, they do begin to respond to interruptions and distractions if their name is called or a visual distraction is offered. At this stage, children still find it difficult to pay attention to a visual and a verbal task at the same time.

- **Attention under voluntary control**, 3–4 years: children begin to control their own focus of attention and can shift this between an activity and the speaker. However, children still have to look at the person speaking.

- **Two-channelled attention**, 4–5 years: children can now move their attention between an activity and a speaker without stopping to look at them. Their attention span may still be short, but children are now ready to pay attention within a group. Children can now attend to a visual and a verbal activity at the same time.

- **Fully integrated attention**, 5 years onwards: children can now carry out a task, focus their attention in various sized groups, ignore distractions and maintain their attention for a reasonable length of time (Reynell, 1980).

It is important to note that not all children will follow these stages rigidly.

Listening to and communicating instructions with children

When taking very young children outdoors, practitioners need to gauge their level of understanding and attention spans. The use of Makaton or picture signs can help children to focus. One setting uses social story books. These are simple picture books using photographs of areas that the child will experience, so they can visualise the experience first. They also include special signs to be used when you want them to focus on an instruction, for example, 'stop', 'look', 'kind hands', 'listening ears', etc. Use of a whistle outdoors, as described in Chapter 3, also can be effective.

Children need to understand instructions and new codes of behaviour that will keep them safe, manage own risks, communicate their needs and for movement in the outdoors.

Time for listening

What is noticeable with young children outside is that they appear more engaged with adults and peers. At first, they play alongside each other and then gradually interact more freely. They learn to take into account each other's thoughts, ideas and feelings. This is a stage from the EYFS, and can also be seen from the Reynell scale for 3–4-year-olds mentioned earlier.

From observations, we have noticed some quieter children seem to relax and build confidence outdoors, particularly when in a smaller group. They speak and engage more with the adults and peers outdoors, than in the nursery. This could be due to a number of reasons. Boys, in particular, are far more engaged with their play when outside. They enjoy the freedom that the outdoors offers them and their focus is improved, due to the additional space and fewer distractions. Research shows that children are much calmer (Forest Research 2005).

Adults usually have more time outdoors to 'really' listen to the child. Sitting or being at the child's eye level allows the child to have your whole attention, rather than catching you as you move from one thing to another. Children recognise the value of an adult's attention. It empowers and raises their self-esteem. It also allows the adult to build their relationship with the child.

Adults are fully engaged with children's ideas in their play, as more time is available for listening

Children talking

The National Strategies for Early Years guidance – *Every Child a Talker* (ECAT) (Department for Education 2008) showed how the spoken language combined with enhanced environments can have significant positive effects upon children's language skills. This strategy worked alongside the UK's EYFS key areas of *the unique child*; including *positive relationships, enabling environments* and *learning and development* and is still widely used now. It has enabled practitioners to audit their settings by seeing how and where language and communication by the children were taking place. The phrase 'Talking hotspots' was used and practitioners were able to use these observations to support their children as it highlighted where gaps presented themselves.

This attractive space was created at the back of a flowerbed planted with large shrubs

Children are aware of their surroundings and learn to use appropriate language

During their snack at Forest School, two children were chatting; earlier the adult had told them that a robin visited the area. Some crumbs had been left out.

G. – 'Ssh we need to have little voices in case Mr. Robin comes.'

J. – 'Where is he?'

G. – 'He's up there, if we have little voices he won't make his Oh-Oh-Oh danger sound, but will do his happy song.'

J. – 'I hear the danger sound over there' – points to another tree.

G. – 'Shhh everyone Mr. Robin is here' – talking to the rest of the group.

Discovering a fallen tree, offers a variety of sensory experiences as children touch and smell the wood. This encouraged the children to use descriptive language. 'It's shiny', 'It's slippery', 'It smells like granddad's

Adults can encourage new language when nature opens up new opportunities

shed'. Some started to talk about how the tree came down and why. 'It didn't like the wind', 'It's sad', 'Will it stand up?'

For example, a small mound near a tree in one outdoor space was seen by the adults as an uninspiring space in need of attention. However, when they observed how the children were using this space in their play, they saw that it was a significant area and decided to leave it alone. A tarpaulin strung between two trees or across a corner with a groundsheet and some cushions or logs makes an attractive space.

Creative spaces and access to a range of open-ended resources enables children to create or re-enact whilst outside. Children with English as an additional language may be reluctant to use English in a larger group but happier with a friend in a small space. A Swedish research article (Norling and Sandberg 2015) found that preschool children play with each other in a different way outside. One staff member stated, 'They have to interact and talk with each other more'; other staff members reported that they encouraged children to make up their own stories in outdoor environments.

First-hand experience

Encouraging children to become aware of their surroundings will offer many communication opportunities. They need to hear adults using creative descriptions of the clouds rushing across the sky, or a small shiny insect scuttling into a safe place. This is particularly important in urban areas. One setting in London is surrounded by blocks of flats but has some trees in its outdoor space.

> M. is watching the Halloween bunting – 'It's moving.'
>
> Adult. – 'Yes the wind is getting stronger.'
>
> M. – 'It's Halloween – the leaves are all golden.'

The outdoor environment provides endless opportunities for metacognitive conversations in which language is constantly challenged and explored. The questions how, what and why can be used so often to stimulate children's learning and understanding. Outdoor experiences, gained at this time, provide children with a resource they can draw on in later life.

Language for questioning

Asking open-ended questions is the most effective way of encouraging the development of children's thought processes. It is important to give them time to respond. Building a relationship with young children is paramount. There needs to be an emotional bond and a sense of mutual trust. As children progress in their spoken language development, the role of language becomes increasingly important in this relationship. Ronald Carter (2004) in his book *Language and Creativity* writes about the function of creative language in sustaining and reinforcing relationships. Playing with words and playing with grammatical and lexical patterns is an important part of this. As children develop their language skills it is interesting to note the way they play with words, sometimes making their own vocabulary. It is important to encourage this playfulness as this is such an effective learning tool. Through play they are exploring and discovering as well as having fun. So many conversations with young children contain made up words but mutual understanding of these reinforces key relationships.

W., aged 18 months, appears to be able to distinguish between sounds and will use a wide range. She uses many recognisable words but has her own words which bear little or no resemblance to the word she hears in her home language. Shoes are referred to as 'De Gores', a cucumber is a 'moon a mumba'. Dinosaurs are 'dolodores', and 'thunderworks' for fireworks.

This playfulness and exploration needs to be encouraged. In time, W. will use the correct words but the ability to create language should be encouraged as far as possible.

Creating poems

Using poetry outdoors is an excellent way to inspire and encourage children to communicate creatively. They need to hear poems and rhymes on a wide range of subjects and an enthusiastic adult will be able to encourage them to use language creatively and compose their own lines or poems. Suitable collections of poems are listed in the resources section at the end of the chapter. The anthology *Exploring Poetry with Young Children* (Watts 2017) contains many poems referring to the natural world and the creatures that can be found within it. It also offers ideas of how to share poetry with children and encourage them to make up their own. Practitioners need to note that poems do not need to rhyme and often the way children put words together, maybe to describe an object or an experience, can be a more creative use of language.

Our role as adults in supporting children's creative communication

In an outdoor environment, there is often more time and space for children to communicate with adults and with each other. There are fewer distractions and children have a natural desire to explore and find out about the world around them.

Children who are given time and enriched environments, particularly those open, wooded or wild areas, will question, work out and communicate with each other as they try to find solutions to their questions or problems within their play. Language development in young children is intricately linked with the development of thought processes. Narrative play is often spontaneous and allows children to explore creative language, its structure, sounds and meanings whilst they play with imaginary worlds, social situations, friendships or conflicts. Such play is drawn from first-hand experiences and from familiar stories, television or films, as mentioned by Rosen (1984, p. 33): 'any story presupposes the existence of other stories'. Adults need to be able to support this development and working with young children outdoors presents many opportunities to fuel their imaginations.

Invite questions when children are observing things in nature – what made the tracks through the pond weed?

An online article by Warren Berger (2012) states that top innovators jumpstart the process of innovation by using the same three words: 'How might we?' There is a subtle difference in the choice of words. By using, 'How can we?' or 'How should we?' there is an implication that maybe we cannot do this, or should we really be doing this? By substituting the word 'might' you will defer judgement which helps people to create options more freely and open up more possibilities. Using this wording is becoming increasingly popular and is very effective. 'It can be seen as a testament to the power of language in helping to spark creative thinking and freewheeling collaboration' (Berger 2012).

Maggie Dugan (n.d.) supports this wording in her online post 'The language of creativity'. She states that the language of creativity tends to be positive and supportive. 'Don't underestimate the impact of language on our creativity. It's amazing how just a few words will put us in the right frame of mind to generate new possibilities.' She suggests we need to pose problems as questions and we believe that this technique should be used with children from a very early age.

POINTS FOR DISCUSSION

■ How much of your interaction with children involves listening to them?

■ What form of questioning do we use outside and are we encouraging children to solve problems for themselves?

■ Do you find that you have areas in your setting where children communicate more freely or have space for quietness or to sit and chat to a friend? If not, what changes if any could you make?

■ Do your practitioners encourage creative poetic and nature language when outdoors?

■ How might we encourage parents to take children outside and talk to them about what they see and hear?

Storytelling

Listening to a story is a special shared experience between the storyteller and the child. A child's imagination begins to develop with the repetition of stories, be they familiar traditional fairy tales and fables, or the wealth of children's literature now available.

In this section, we will look at:

■ how to support children's listening skills

■ how to develop vocabulary and imaginative language

■ how children's storytelling and narrative storying can be valued

■ how adults can be better storytellers.

Listening to stories with and without books

Many children's stories like the 'Gruffalo', or 'Stickman' or 'Going on a Bear Hunt' draw from the environment of woodlands and are ideal to re-enact or tell. Repetition of any story is hugely important for early years' children. A story is re-enacted in their play as they work through it, learning about its meaning and introducing new ideas, thoughts and storylines.

Nancy Mellon in her book *Storytelling with Children* mentions that 'it can take weeks, even months until that mysterious moment when a child is satisfied and ready to move on'. She goes

Providing areas outside for children to enjoy books can allow them to enjoy familiar stories anywhere

on to say that every child needs to build 'strength, stability and security' before they can fully understand the meaning behind any story (Mellon 2000, p. 31).

Taking these well-known stories outdoors makes them come alive. Children will find places and artefacts that fit the criteria for characters, homes, transport and props to support the story in their play. Take for example the story of the three little pigs. By encouraging den building, children have the freedom to move around a large environment making different homes, finding places to hide as the wolf or perhaps include a home for the wolf. Making props to use in the 'homes' and pretending to cook a meal on a campfire all become part of their play. Providing a real experience, such as cooking on an open fire, helps the story become embedded into the child's consciousness.

Many stories can be connected with the landscape, seasons, animals or promote an understanding of conservation and caring for the environment. There are also many that will involve woodland fairies, dragons, goblins and folklore from around the world. A few examples can be found in the appendix to this chapter, along with internet links to other sources.

Taking familiar stories outside to read to children throughout the day encourages creative language and rhyme. Adults can also use simple natural objects as props – here a small stick becomes a wand

CASE STUDY: THE THREE BILLY GOATS GRUFF

A group of children at a local nursery first used a variety of loose parts within the nursery setting to act out the story, before taking it out further into their Forest School areas.

The children had access to:

■ *a selection of wigs for the 'troll' to wear*

■ *tabards with goat features on them,*

■ *a selection of large blocks, planks, crates, ropes and other miscellaneous items.*

The children were really taken with the story and would make a variety of different structures. At first it was a simple bridge structure, but over the weeks this structure became more elaborate, involving other areas which the 'Billy goats' needed to negotiate when they told their version of the story. The 'Troll' was also given more resources to hide behind.

A. – 'this can be the grablulator', he was referring to an old hosepipe, rope and wooden reel, which was going to catch things.

G. – 'Put it here, then it will catch them.'

A. – 'No it needs to go here', moving it to the stage area.

Making use of settings resources if you are not able to access wood or parkland spaces

G. – 'Let's put this here too', moving a long plank to the stage area and trying to balance it on a smaller block.

F. – who has been watching the first two boys, joins in, 'this go here', bringing a larger block.

A. – 'Yes we need more.'

F. goes and gets more and adds to the pile.

A. – 'We need to put them like this', moving them into a long line, when they had been stacked.

G. – 'I got this big one' and puts it further away near a sloping block.

F. – Then goes and gets another long plank and places it on the blocks to cover the gap. 'There that's good it works.'

Building continued for some time. In retelling their version of the story, two of the children shouted out the phrase 'Who's that trip trapping on my bridge?'

They let the two smaller goats over, but in their version of the story, they capture the bigger goat.

Following this, the group went out on one of their Forest School sessions, and used one of the many fallen trees that they are used to going across as the bridge for the story and their version was played out again, this time in the woods.

A fallen tree becomes the perfect bridge

Adults as the storyteller

In Forest School, there is a tradition of oral storytelling and traditional tales are shared at practitioners' gatherings and handed on to others. A good storyteller can weave all the sights, sounds and even smells that are around to spark the imagination of the child, bringing a story to life.

First create a special space and 'atmosphere'. Will there be dragons, goblins, giants or fairies? What lands will we see? Will there be sadness, adventure and happy endings?

For very young children knowing the simple well-known phrases to start the story helps the child to focus and listen to the storyteller. Use simple phrases like 'Once upon a time. . .', or 'This is a tale of magic and mystery from a time long ago. . .'.

Some storytellers use a number of props; those who play the guitar or ukulele can bring songs into their tale. Simple chords throughout will add to the atmosphere and focus the children's attention. A professional storyteller inspired several practitioners when he came to a Forest School Association gathering and introduced a 'Hapi Drum'. The sound and rhythm was mesmerising as he used it to bring the group together and start his tale. He would then use it as a beginning to a new part of the tale, changing the volume as he played, keeping the group enthralled throughout.

The use of movement, vocal expression and eye contact to tell the tale is very important. Learning the story from beginning to end, and being ready to adjust accordingly is key to engaging with the audience, and enables you, the storyteller, to be confident and relaxed.

A Hapi drum can be used with beaters or just hands to provide rhythmic addition to any story

Natural materials that are lying around can be used to illustrate stories or in an end of session reflection. With a little imagination, a small twig, leaves and long grass to use as binding or an elastic band, can represent one of your children or a creature that was encountered during the session. It does not need to be perfect and you will find children will appreciate its simplicity as they use their own imaginations.

Keeping the attention of your young audience is an art that comes from experience and a great deal of trial and error. Having several techniques up your sleeve is key for any good storyteller. Knowing your story inside out is crucial and allows you to be flexible as you adapt your story to meet the language needs of your group.

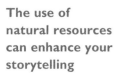

The use of natural resources can enhance your storytelling

Types of stories that are particularly good for outside environments include:

- traditional fairy tales and fables

- tree-related tales from 'spirit of trees' website (see 'Useful resources' below)

- international stories – for example, Native American, African, Maori or Aboriginal

- environmental stories – stories that encourage children to care for the wildlife and the earth

- compassionate stories – stories that show children love, caring and understanding in a variety of situations

- reflective stories at the end of your session.

Children as story makers

Children will refer to familiar scenarios in their play, which range from home life, families, animals and holidays to superheroes and television characters. Children use play as a means of working things out and finding answers to questions. Much of this type of play takes place in the nursery environment and will continue and develop outdoors. Natural forms in the outside environment can become anything in a child's imagination.

Natural forms in the environment can become anything in the child's imagination. This moss covered stone becomes the shop as the family take on roles of shopkeeper, supplier and customer

Roleplay familiar roles using language they understand and know, with the use of resources around them for their props. Practitioners can use creative language to extend learning and to enable those with limited language to participate

Recording children's stories and play narratives

There have been many studies on recording and valuing children's storytelling and narratives to their play. Vivian Gussin Paley looked at this in detail, and goes on to say 'this view of play makes play, along with its alter ego, storytelling and story acting, the universal learning medium' (Paley 1990, p. 10).

During a project in Surrey known as 'Creative Shoots' in 2015 a professional artist introduced early years practitioners to the work of Vivian Gussin Paley using 'Helicopter storying' (Surrey County Council 2015; Paley 1990). Practitioners were able to put this concept into practice, with the use of the 'story acting box' and various methods of allowing children's language and storytelling to be valued and recorded. Children would tell a story which was scribed word for word and then they were invited to act out the story. A special place is marked out on the floor (using tape indoors or sticks outside). The child actor enters the space and re-enacts his tale inviting other children as necessary to join in and to enter the space.

This concept enables children to create new language, as well as their own movements and interpretation of the characters. Practitioners should not direct how the children move, or what they should say. Tricia Lee in her book *Princesses, Dragons and Helicopter Stories* (Lee 2016, p. 13) recalls having to sit on her hands to avoid them gesticulating types of movement. She was then able to observe the tiniest movement and sound of a very quiet child's fingers acting out throwing and catching her ball. She then copied the child's tiny movement which valued that child's contribution.

Claire Waldon, from Mindstretchers, uses a floorbook to encourage children's questioning, interests and learning. They work together to record particular ideas, stories and interests or to recall something that happened. Floorbooks are regularly used at Peter Pan nursery for creative projects with their local art centre. They are also used for their Forest School sessions. Photographs and drawings are added to recall particular activities and children's stories. New ideas are then followed up with the children.

When children go outdoors their narrative storying and their imaginative storytelling can be taken to a new level. They have to think about what they can use for their props, find areas of play, build structures for their play, and incorporate new story lines. These new areas, will often take on new 'location names' by the children; with one group a particular tree became the 'crocodile', and children throughout the setting (even those who had not attended that session) knew about the adventures of this 'crocodile'.

Using a floorbook with children, talking about their adventures, which the children then add to with their drawings; here the setting has sourced colouring pencils made from sticks. Their ideas are added and scribed by practitioners

CASE STUDY: STORY OF THE CROCODILE

A group of children (aged from 3½ to 4½) attending a Forest School session soon become confident with the area, expectations and routine of Forest School. The children were introduced to new ways of building, hunting for resources, and using the tools and items in their 'trolley' known as 'trundle dog'.

Some children in this group were quieter than a couple of the children, who were at first, quite dominating. The practitioners would allow the whole group opportunities for each child to lead through the woodland, to find and make things in their own time. The children would often work either alone or in smaller groups. Over time, the children were able to see each other's strengths, and worked with each other instead of alongside.

Over several weeks the children gradually learnt to accept each other's needs, and gained the skills of listening to and communicating with each other. One area of the site that they were particularly fascinated with was a fairly new fallen tree; this was in its process of decaying and would often have birch polypore fungus growing on parts, which became fascinating to look at and study. Where the tree trunk had fallen and snapped, it had opened up the inside of the trunk, showing the flesh and where animals had taken advantage of the new area for food and shelter. The root system was still intact with some roots slightly raised and covered with moss. The children would often refer to this tree, as 'the crocodile'. This soon became a continued story theme every time they came to the area.

The children have formed secure relationships in order to listen and take into consideration everyone's views without the intervention of an adult

Towards the end of the autumn term the children had become so confident in each other's abilities that they would now work as a team, planning, introducing new story lines of what had happened to 'the crocodile' and were making 'medicine' for 'the crocodile' – who now had a number of imaginary ailments from tooth ache to sore legs.

Each child had a role to play; they would communicate with each other about what was happening to the crocodile, giving suggestions about what they could find or do. Some made use of the tools and took on the role of a doctor. Food would be prepared and 'cooked' on their imaginary open fire. During each visit to the area they would remember and recall events from their story and then continue their play.

One of the scenarios was the 'crocodile's sore legs'. The children felt the moss was the cause and are using their tools to remove it

Having discussed their plans everyone has a job to do and knows exactly what needs doing

We can see how children develop over time with adult support. Being in a small group, they had lots of opportunity to talk and be listened to. Tina Bruce talks about the adult as the informed observer, and she mentions that it is important for the adult to appreciate and value the beginnings of the children's creativity without taking over (Bruce 2011). It was clear that the practitioner during the final stages of the children's play took no role other than an observer, as children had gained sufficient confidence to work together.

Following the involvement with the Creative Shoots Project this year, staff noticed increased levels of creative thinking and storytelling.

Since this initial observation, having experienced a whole year of Forest School, children were now to become 'Mentors' to the younger children for the last few weeks of the school year. They would show them everything about Forest School that they had learnt, including the two areas where Forest School took place.

One important piece of knowledge that the children were very keen to impart was 'the crocodile'. They explained in great detail about what type of food it needed, showed them where the ferns were – which was the 'food', and which was the 'sore leg', pointing to the particular root with moss that needed to be scraped off. The new children soon became involved in their game.

In the autumn term these younger children experienced their first full Forest School session. With no clues or hints from the adults, the children recognised the fallen tree structure that the previous year's Forest School group had introduced to them. Several children immediately started to find leaves to feed it and started to develop different stories involving the 'crocodile' in their play.

The new group now continues the story of the crocodile with new ideas for the play – this time he has a sore tummy

This verbal storytelling skill has been used for centuries and is how traditional, native and local tales continue over the years. The children here are keeping this skill alive. It will be interesting to see how the story continues as the tree trunk decays and whether the children will then go and find a different area or structure to continue this play.

Young children and storytelling

For some very young children, a wider open-ended environment makes it harder for them to imagine these 'imaginary play areas'. The use of small toys or play props can help. Every teddy will need a little house or a hammock for bedtime, a toy bird will need a nest to be kept safe. Having structures either in place or part built can help to further their communication or story language. The adult's role is to use creative language for children to hear, repeat or mimic. Talk about the children's actions and use language to describe them, for example, if they carry a teddy through the trees, it could sound like, 'Teddy and Jo go creeping through the woods' or 'walking through the woodland what do I see? . . . I see Katie and teddies coming too'. The latter example is a phrase adapted from the rhyme 'Walking through the jungle' and repeated will encourage them to copy you or make up their own as they learn new words and sounds. Adults can also use these methods with children whose English is an additional language.

Provocations for children's imagination and storytelling

A provocation is something that provokes thoughts, ideas and creative discussion. It can simply be a small object, note, or even a partially built structure. (See Golden Egg case study in Chapter 5.) In one setting, practitioners left a witches' recipe for apple spiders, one child found some mud and sticks and made his own spider for the recipe.

Using a witches' spell the child was able to then create a spider for his play

The apple spider

With a little imagination, adults can leave particular items for open-ended play or that refer to a well-known story. When leaving an object, check the area carefully for any unwanted rubbish or manmade items that could cause harm to the children. It is also advisable to remove the provocation item at the end of your session if you are on public land.

What story would a small bowl and spoon, a treasure box, a pair of small boots, or magical stick tell? By placing any one of these examples you can provide a new line of enquiry to the children's play

Another provocation is the 'talking tin' as shown with the case study in Chapter 5. This is a small recording device that can hold a sound or message for children to listen to and act upon.

These small devices are another form of provocation and a short message can be recorded for the children to hear and then act upon. Alternatively, they can use them to record their own sounds

Conclusion

A rich environment and opportunities for children to converse are key to developing confident and able talkers. Dummies and modern technologies all can have a negative impact on children's speech and ability to communicate. Adults also need to remember to give the child the time to respond. All too often an answer is given far too quickly for the child; but a child who has language and processing difficulties, or a child whose English is not their first language, needs extra time to think through what is being asked of them and then be able to work out a response. Creative language and poetry needs to be embraced by adults, for early years' children to become creative talkers.

Telling verbal stories was slowly becoming a lost art form, but many places are now turning to bringing in the local 'storyteller' to their centre or places of interest. In the UK, the National Trust, historic venues and the Eden Project in Cornwall have regular resident storytellers, to bring history, local culture or environmental issues come alive. Adults also need to become confident in their storytelling abilities, and stretch further into unfamiliar tales from local fables or those tales from around the world. By encouraging storytelling and story acting throughout the day and in different outdoor environments, children's imaginations and love for storytelling are enhanced, and children are required to engage both cognitively and socially with their peers. Children will then weave elements from their daily lives and from the literary world into their own stories. As Vygotsky (1967, p. 9) stated, 'what passes unnoticed by the child in real life becomes a rule of behaviour in play'. This is also true in today's society and the exposure children have to popular cultures via television, film, internet and toys. Many of their stories will have elements from these superheroes, princesses and other known characters.

Being outdoors in an exciting space will enable children to become confident listeners and speakers. They will use language as they find new things to explore every day and develop their thinking skills as they work together to offer ideas for their play and storymaking.

POINTS FOR DISCUSSION

- How might you use 'provocations' in your setting?
- Can you extend the range of stories you use with children, developing your own skills as storytellers and communicators?
- How can you make more use of natural resources in your storytelling?
- Do you give children time to invent and create their own stories and play sequences?

USEFUL RESOURCES

Examples of verbal stories:

- *Mama Africa* (often known in the UK as *Mama Earth*) – African creation story

- *The Perfect House* (perfection is not about possessions or what you look like, but is more to do with your surroundings/community and how you work with them) – original source: *Story-making and Creative Group Work with Older People*, by Paula Crimmens (JKP 1998).

The following tales are from the website www.spiritoftrees.org:

- *The Harper in Fairyland* – tales from an apple tree retold by Beth Vaughan

- *The Lady in White* (silver birch tale) retold by Cristy West

Books and websites

Cultivating Creativity in Toddlers by Tina Bruce (Hodder)

Going on a Bear Hunt by Michael Rosen (Walker Books)

The Gruffalo and *Stickman* by Julia Donaldson (Macmillan Children's Books)

The Giving Tree by Shel Silverstein (Penguin books)

The Storyteller's Way by Ashley Ramsden and Sue Hollingsworth (Hawthorn Press)

Storytelling for a Greener World by A. Gersie, A. Nanson, E. Schieffelin, C. Collinson and J. Cree (Hawthorn Press)

The Lost Words by Robert Macfarlane and Jackie Morris (Penguin Books)

www.mindstretchers.co.uk – floor books, Claire Waldon

Bibliography

Berger, W. (2012) 'The secret phrase top innovators use', *Harvard Business Review*, 17 September, online article at https://hbr.org/2012/09/the-secret-phrase-top-innovato.

Bruce, T. (2011) *Cultivating Creativity*. London: Hodder Education.

Carter, Ronald (2004) *Language and Creativity: The Art of Common Talk*. London: Routledge.

Cremin, T. (2017) *Storytelling in Early Childhood*. London: Routledge.

Department for Education (2008) *National Strategies in Early Years – 'Every child a talker'* (ECAT), available at: http://webarchive.nationalarchives.gov.uk/20130321061204/https://www.education.gov.uk/publications/eOrderingDownload/DCSF-00854-2008.pdf.

Dugan, Maggie (n.d.) 'The Language of Creativity', blog, available at: https://knowinnovation.com/2015/07/the-language-of-creativity/.

Forest Research (2005) *An Evaluation of Forest School in England*. Report available at: https://www.forestry. gov.uk/website/pdf.nsf/pdf/ForestSchoolEnglandReport.pdf/$FILE/ForestSchoolEnglandReport.pdf

Lee, T. (2016) *Princesses, Dragons and Helicopter Stories*. London: Routledge.

Mellon, N. (2000). *Storytelling with Children*. Stroud: Hawthorn Press.

Norling, M. and Sandberg, A. (2015) 'Language learning in outdoor environments: Perspectives of preschool staff', *Nordic Early Childhood Education Research Journal* 9(1): 1–16. https://journals.hioa. no/index.php/nbf/article/view/749.

Paley, V.G. (1990) *The Boy who Would be a Helicopter: The Uses of Storytelling in the Classroom*. Cambridge, MA: Harvard University Press.

Reynell, J. (1980) *Language Development and Assessment*. Dordrecht: Springer.

Rosen, H. (1984) *Stories and Meanings*. Sheffield: National Association for the Teaching of English.

Surrey County Council (2015) Early Years 'Creative Shoots'.

Vygotsky, L.S. (1967) 'Play and its role in the mental development of the child', *Soviet Psychology* 12: 6–18 (translation of a lecture delivered in Russian in 1933).

Watts, A. (2017) *Exploring Poetry with Young Children*. London: Routledge.

Appendix

- 'The story of Mama Africa' (Creation story), adapted here by Julie Johnson

- 'The story of the perfect house'

- 'The story of the forget-me-not flower'

The story of Mama Africa

(You can change to your own town/country or earth. In this adaptation we refer to 'Mama Earth'.) An oral story that originates from Africa and is an alternative creation story.

Many moons ago, when the earth was dark and lonely, Mama Earth woke up and decided it was too dark, so she rubbed her hands together and a spark came and lit up the earth with lots of little lights in the sky, she called them stars. *(If you are able to, use a fire steel to create sparks here.)* She then made a bigger spark and this she called the moon but it was still not quite bright enough, so she made a huge spark – this she called the sun. She put the moon at the bottom of the earth and the sun at the top, and saw they could spin around giving the earth different shades of light. Mama Earth was happy and went back to sleep.

Mama Earth woke up and could see the earth was still in need of something. So she thought and thought and then put her hands into the soil and clay and created some strange shapes, some tall, some small, some with lots of spikes, and some with soft leaf and petal shapes. She blew on them and put them on the ground. She sat back and watched as the shapes took hold of the earth and grew into beautiful trees and bushes, some with all different shaped leaves and some with flowers; some even had fruit that could be eaten.

Mama Earth was pleased and went back to sleep.

When she woke up again, she felt something else was needed. She looked around and thought and thought, then she put her hands into the earthen clay and pulled some out. Then she found

**Creature made after the story
Mama Earth**

some twigs and leaves and things that were lying on the ground and put them into the clay. *(At this point the adult telling the story will have some modelling clay and can pick up any natural object off the ground that is nearby.)*

She started to make all different types of things. Some looked as if they had legs, some with wing shapes, some with eyes and mouths and some with none. When she was finished she picked each one up and blew on it – through magical sparkles, it then changed and became real. Some went off into the trees, some along the ground, some flew into the sky and some even went into the rivers and seas.

Mama Earth was very pleased and she went back to sleep for a long rest after all her hard work.

(You can either finish the story here and then give the children their own piece of clay to make their own bug or creature – inviting them to give it a name – no matter how strange it may seem. Alternatively you can then continue by introducing humans to the story, adding how she taught them how to care for the creatures and all the things that lived on the earth and in the waters.)

★

The story of the perfect house

Original source: Storymaking and Creative Groupwork with Older People, Paula Crimmens, JKP 1998. (Adapted for use at Peter Pan Nursery during the Creative Shoots Project 2013 by Roya Hamid and here by Julie Johnson.)

In a village that had seen great loss and sadness, two brothers and their sister who had lost their parents built their own house, 'The Perfect House', in their minds. They had a party to celebrate its completion. During the party an old lady arrived (who missed out on the invitations to the party). When asked what she thought of their perfect house, she replied that it wasn't.

It needed three things, the Water of Life, the Tree of Knowledge and the Singing Bird – all of which could be found up the big mountain, which was guarded by the Giant. She leaves them with an old knife, saying 'in times of trouble it will start to rust'.

The story continues with the eldest brother Steven going off to find the items. When he arrived at the mountain he was confronted by the Giant. The Giant says that he can continue but tells him 'Don't look left, don't look right and don't look behind'. Steven continues. When hearing noises and voices from the left and the right he remembers the Giant's words, but forgets when he hears what he thought was his younger brother's voice from behind calling his name, 'Steven, Steven'. He turns and is turned to stone.

Back at the house the knife starts to rust. The younger brother, David, heads out. Not as strong as his older brother, he takes a bit longer to get there. He meets the Giant and hears what he has to say. He then continues up the mountain. He too is turned to stone when he forgets and looks to the right when he thinks he hears his brother calling him. Again, the knife gets some more rust.

Seeing the rusty knife, the young sister, Hollie, then builds up the courage to go and look for them. Her persona is small, not very strong but wise. She packs food and a jug to collect water to drink. Her journey is much harder and longer, in fact over several days. She meets the Giant, but she is tired and hungry. She sits down and offers the giant some of her food which he gratefully accepts. Remembering the Giant's words she heads up the mountain. It was a difficult journey. Occasionally she received cuts and scratches from rocks and thorns from bushes. She remembers the Giant's words and does not look left or right or behind, even when she hears familiar voices, some of which sounded like her brothers.

When at the top, she sees the Tree of Knowledge and the Water of Life. She is tired and thirsty and takes a drink from the water; she then washes her face including her long hair and as she swishes up her hair the water droplets fall onto all the various rocks around her. Suddenly, each one then turns back to a human who had once travelled up the mountain and got lost, including her two brothers and their parents.

The child is being the 'Giant' and reciting the words 'don't look left, don't look right and don't look behind'. By finding this fallen tree structure the children felt this was perfect for the Giant to stand upon as it meant the children were then bigger than the adults around them

In the tree, she hears the singing bird. Being a wise girl she asked the Giant if he could help her bring the tree down to the village. She fills her jug with water, gives the bird some food, who then flies down with them. Back at the village another party is held to celebrate the return of the lost villagers and the brave and wise little girl.

This time the old lady is invited and she said that it was indeed the Perfect House, because of the community and the experiences they had.

★

The story of the forget-me-not flower

(As heard by Chris Salisbury at the FSA Conference 2016 and adapted here by Julie Johnson.)

Long ago, there was a village which was suffering troubles far and wide, and where the annual rains had disappeared. One day the Village Chief asked each villager to find something of value to them to give to the fire gods in order to please them and to bring the rains so their crops would grow. Some brought jewels. Some brought grain and goats, but then a small child came forward and brought her carved doll.

The elders asked the child why she brought this doll, which was looking very shabby and worn. The child explained that the doll held many stories of all the people she loved.

Firstly, the doll was carved by her father. When he was out for many days gathering food for the family, he carved this from a small stick that he found when resting from the heat of the sun. The small cloth that was wrapped around the doll was woven by her mother who sang sweet songs as she weaved. The wool that was used to spin into thread for her to weave the cloth was collected by her sisters and brothers as they played and laughed. The wool was then teased and spun by her grandma, who told her stories from long ago.

The elders listened and agreed that this was a very special gift and allowed the child to put her wooden carved doll with the memories of everyone who was special to her into the fire.

The fire grew and the flames looked as if they were dancing with joy. The fire gods were indeed pleased and sent the rains to the village. Then after the rains had stopped, the gods sent a new gift, that of a special flower known as the 'forget-me-not'. This now reminds the villagers to remember that their most valued possession is their family and the stories they hear with them throughout their lives.

★

5 Creative structures and design in the natural world

As children design and build large and small structures, they will be working in all areas of learning. They will be developing strength and coordination, learning about length, weight and height and using language to communicate their ideas to others. Adults can extend their knowledge as they discuss how various structures have been built through the ages

In this chapter you will:

- ■ gain an understanding of the reasons and benefits of building small and large structures in the outdoor environment

- ■ be aware of safety points to consider for gathering natural materials in the outdoor environment

- ■ be aware of the safety points to consider when building large structures

- ■ gain some ideas to support emergent structure building with babies and children under three in the outdoor environment

- ■ gain some ideas on how to use structure building to support imaginative development with children three to six

- ■ look at the ways adults interact with children to support their learning

- ■ look at areas to reflect upon with your own practice and working environment.

Creative structures and areas of learning

Characteristics of effective learning have been outlined in Chapter 1 and here we look more closely at how the use of natural materials to build with enables children to develop these characteristics of learning.

When building structures children need to think what they need, find the materials and then know how to adapt or change the materials to fit in with their design. They may not be able to envisage the end result, but with support of the adult and help from each other they will build and adapt the materials as they work together. As the work progresses they will begin to think critically and share ideas to improve or make something work better. If they are building a shelter they may begin to use other materials such as moss or bracken to cover it. They may decide it could be a house, a fort or a cave. The list is endless and limited only by the child's imagination.

Building in an outdoor environment will enable children to do this freely, without being confined to a small space, or have interruptions from others. It will allow for learning in the three prime areas: personal, social and emotional development; physical movement; and communication and language.

Personal, social and emotional development is stimulated in various ways. As we observe children, we become aware of the different ways they interact with each other according to the situations they are in. A young toddler may be nervous of an outdoor space if it is their first experience, but with adult support will develop confidence and begin to explore the environment in a variety of ways. Older children may operate independently in the space, but usually when building structures they are working in a group and need to negotiate and discuss with each other. A shy child may suddenly become confident and have an idea that will be taken on by the group.

Physical movement is encouraged, as collection of materials will need to be hunted for and moved to the building area. Children need to develop the skill of moving round an uneven forest floor avoiding brambles, sticks and other hazards. They need to use their whole bodies to carry logs and sticks and manipulate them into position to form the structure. Research indicates that physical movement has a positive impact on brain development (Goddard Blythe 2011). The physical challenges will therefore enhance the children's levels of critical thinking and judgement as they place materials to form their structure.

Communication and language can also be stimulated. Practitioners will see several opportunities when working in the outdoors environment and in particular on a project when they need to work together. Case studies will show how children use language to express ideas and to negotiate with others.

The four specific areas of learning are also enhanced.

Literacy is encouraged, particularly when children design structures for animals or mythical creatures. They will be using reference books to source knowledge and practitioners can use story characters to stimulate children's imagination. They may be inventing stories of their own as they work on these projects.

Mathematics features highly in this area of creativity. Estimating the length of a stick and working out whether it is a suitable shape, size and length for the purpose are key elements in successful structure building. They will be looking at angles, height and space when building structures and working out how elements can fit together.

Understanding the world – building structures for a purpose helps to contribute to this area of learning. Homes for animals will encourage children to find out more about creatures and habitats. Children may want to learn more about how bridges were built through the centuries. Why were they needed? Building a raft too, can lead to children finding out about earlier civilisations and how they travelled.

Expressive arts and design is another area of learning that features highly in these activities. Designing for a purpose comes in at a very early stage. Toddlers may be asked to build a bed for their doll or teddy. With support they will be able to choose appropriate materials, moss or bracken for example, and then look at making a bed of appropriate size. They may be able to add collected items to their structure and older children will certainly be able to enhance their structures in many expressive ways.

Small structure building

Practitioner preparation

The first task of any practitioner is to know what natural resources you can access and have an understanding of the outdoor area that you use in the various seasons. Wet and cold weather can provide just as many exciting opportunities for learning as warm, dry days; adults and children alike just need to be dressed appropriately. Look at naturally sheltered areas in your outdoor environment which may be suitable for this activity.

If you have access to woodland spaces consider:

- the number of trees and types – are they all one species or is there a mixture, e.g. oak, birch, or hazel? Are there small plants like ferns, rhododendron bushes, bamboo, and holly?

- whether you have permission to coppice anything in your area

- supplies of small collecting materials – acorns, fir cones, sticks, blossom, and grasses?

- if you have areas that fill with water – puddles, ponds or streams?

- whether the area you use is private or public land and do you have permission to use it?

- how you support children not to pick flowers.

If you have access to an area that is limited with natural resources consider the following:

- Are you able to bring in natural resources yourself or can members of your community help?

- Do you have local places that you are able to visit, and/or that you could recommend to your families to visit? Could you use these venues for whole family events?

■ Can you link up with any local wildlife or woodland type groups?

■ If none of the above is available to you, are you able to adapt an area of your outdoor space in your setting?

Practitioners' Safety Points

Always be aware of any natural items that can cause harm. Make sure you show the children these items and give them instructions in a way that they can understand, and the message of 'no touching, leave these for birds and animals'. Remember the rule of 'fingers out of mouths when outside at Forest School'.

Plants to avoid:

■ Holly berries

■ Toadstools

■ Stinging nettles

■ Laburnum seeds

■ Foxgloves

If you are unsure, there are a number of websites and books that can help you. Stinging nettles, however, are an interesting plant, as they can also be used to make twine and tea among other things. It is often said 'once bitten, twice shy' and this applies to this plant; children are quick to recognise them and this becomes part of the risk taking that children will learn.

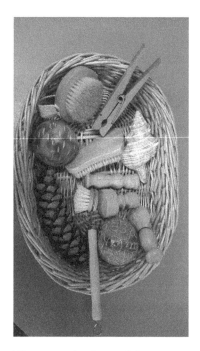

Building small structures with the under-threes

In this section, we will look at ways that younger children can be involved in some of the building process and look at their emergent creative ideas. The section also looks at ways in which adults, can encourage further creative thinking.

Babies learn quickly by using all their senses and will explore their environment in a variety of ways. It is important to offer a wide variety of sensory and exploratory experiences from an early age. The use of treasure baskets with babies is well-documented as a way to do this.

Treasure basket with natural items

Treasure basket with metal items

Children up to the age of eighteen months spend time deconstructing rather than constructing. At twelve months old, a baby systematically crawled on the beach following a line of sand pies that had been made for her, knocking them down one by one. Similarly, children will enjoy knocking down towers or scattering objects in a random fashion. However, from eighteen months with adult support they are able to begin to construct. Small towers can be built and they will enjoy helping to make the sand pies as well as knocking them down.

You can begin to encourage the use of natural materials in building. Make a pile of sticks of similar length and thickness. Lay three down on the ground as a base and then encourage the child to add another three. Working together you can build a small tower structure. You may want to sit a Humpty Dumpty figure on top and sing the nursery rhyme 'Humpty Dumpty sat on a wall'. Children will enjoy helping Humpty to fall and then rebuilding the wall if necessary to repeat the song.

Young children love to collect, and this will encourage their participation in emergent building. When collecting small natural materials, natural

Using sticks to build towers

baskets are really good for this, but any type of bag or container will give a sense of ownership to their collections.

Whatever type of setting you are in, it is important to make a space for children's collections. This can simply be a special place on the ground. It could be marked out with natural materials if you wish or it could be the level stump of a fallen tree or log if you have one. Children will begin to display their collections and they will be able to use some of their items to enhance small structures. A piece of bark can be decorated with grass or petals to make a boat. Humpty's wall can be enhanced with nuts or seeds or whatever the children find.

Building to develop imagination and role play

As children begin to develop their imagination, so too will they develop their role play. At first, it may be that they can collect some straw, moss or grasses and make a simple pillow or bed and lie down on it themselves. They may be able to work with an adult and begin to place the moss and grass in an appropriate place. Encouraging them to make a bed for their favourite teddy or doll can develop this idea. Encourage the toddler to help you, and then gradually reduce your input when they are at a stage of building independently. You could build alongside them, narrating your actions in your build and also theirs, like this:

'I think I will place this stick here, oh I see you did . . . that's clever.'

'Will my teddy fit in here, let me see . . . mmm I need to make it bigger, oh your teddy fits just fine ...'

Children will begin to experiment with natural materials at this stage; they will use a stick to poke in mud, they might watch a leaf or a piece of bark floating on a puddle. If you offer them a simple square of twigs lashed together at the corners and some appropriate sized twigs, they may be able to build a small raft and decorate it with some of their collected items. Watching their own raft floating on a puddle will encourage a sense of pride in their own creation. As an adult you are laying the foundations for them to use natural materials in ever increasing ways.

Building small structures with children over three

Building animal homes

When building animal homes you will first need to ensure that they have some basic knowledge about the creatures and the type of homes they live in. This can either be done with real objects, or showing children where to find this information from books or the Internet.

Small plastic or soft animal/bird toys can be introduced for children to use to build their structures. This gives them an idea of the size of the structure they need to make in order for

This family used stones and other found items on a beach to make a home for their toy puppy

these toys to fit inside. Children may be observed undertaking a variety of roles, from designer, supervisor or collector, children working independently or working together. A good story to read is *After the Storm* by Nick Butterworth. This looks at the different kinds of animals in need of new homes after a big storm destroyed their habitat.

Keeping small items like these wooden birds in your pocket can enable spur of the moment structure building

During the season different materials can be added

CASE STUDY: THE GOLDEN EGG

As part of a creative project in one nursery, staff left out 'Golden Eggs' (made from polystyrene) for the children to find firstly within the nursery garden. One egg was then left in the woods and children were encouraged to build a nest, which would keep the egg safe and dry. They made a nest under a bush to protect it from rain and predators.

B. – 'Look guys, look!'

I. – 'It's an egg, is it hatching?'

B. – 'No it's lost its mummy.'

Iz. – 'It needs a nest.'

B. – 'Guys, guys we need lots of leaves and sticks' – talking to the boys nearby.

J. – 'Here's some' – handing over some silver birch sticks and a piece of bark.

B. – 'That's like a roof to stop it getting wet.'

I. – 'I've got some moss for the bed.'

The children continue building the nest and then place the egg carefully onto the moss and leaves; one child finds the large piece of silver birch and places this partly over the egg. The children are working together as they see a real need of urgency for this egg which could contain a small creature. They are showing real care for its wellbeing, with the need to protect it from the weather and the fact the mother was not there.

The children are discussing their find of the golden egg, and what they should do to protect it

Building small structures for mythological creatures

As children develop their imagination and are introduced to a variety of colourful and imaginative storybooks, they become more interested in ideas about imaginary beings and creatures. Children will come up with a whole range of ideas, and fairies, dragons and unicorns often feature in their conversations. Practitioners should encourage the conversations and could then ask questions about the creatures. Children will enjoy creating homes and will often surprise the adults by their inventiveness. Initially they may need support and adults need to ensure a wide variety of materials are available.

You may need to show them where to find materials that are around them and how to build a small 'lean-to' type structure, then allow them to create their own ideas, supporting when needed and not doing the actual building for them.

Get children to think of different types of buildings that these mythical creatures might need:

- homes
- school or nursery
- bakery
- jam making factory
- magic potion supplies shop
- wing repair shop
- fairy castle.

The list is endless and the children will soon start to think of others

There may be an old tree trunk or a hole in the ground near your setting that will stimulate the imagination. Children will begin to discuss what creatures might be living there. They might begin by adding some leaves or making a mossy bed in the hole for a creature.

This old tree stump has become a popular place for the child to construct a home for the woodland fairies, finding items for beds, cups and pieces of bark for tables

Over time various additions are added by other children

A frame structure

A tepee structure

Semi-dome structure

With small structures, children are learning different design techniques as well as the valuable lesson of 'cause and effect'. Repeating the same move enables the brain to fully understand that a new position of placing the stick needs to be tried to give better results. This small building skill will often be used later in life in a number of occupations.

The basic lean-to type structure is an easy one to grasp initially as most will be able to find a good area at the base of any tree that could become a 'home'; you can introduce an A-frame or tepee type structure and then more elaborate self-supporting dome structures as they develop their building skills.

Using a 'talking tin', children can be left simple messages which can enhance or extend their play. In the following case study, the children were asked to help the woodland fairies build some safe buildings as the mummy and baby dragon had squashed their buildings when they came by.

CASE STUDY: TALKING TIN

Two children found a small bag, which contained a 'Talking tin' – a small recording device. The children were used to these as they are often used in nursery and the children knew how to operate it. They listened to the message which was from the 'Queen of the Fairies', telling the children that a mummy dragon and baby dragon were out in the woods but had unfortunately squashed some of the fairy houses as they accidentally sat on them while listening to their bed time story. The fairies would love it if the children could help them to rebuild their homes.

The two children told some of the other children in the group about the message and told them they needed to help. Each child started to gather different sticks and leaves, and chose to build their structure, some of the boys needed more support with the task, and were content with collecting the materials for others, but less interested in building detailed structures. The two girls decided to build their home under a holly bush as the prickles would prickle the dragon's bottom.

This was a simple activity, where the adult supported the children with some of the collecting, but encouraged the children to come up with their own ideas. The two girls clearly had a plan of protecting the fairies from the dragons with their idea of building under the holly bush.

Building small items to extend imaginative play

Other items can be introduced to encourage and support their imaginative play. Children will enjoy creating and using a fishing rod, boats/rafts, a magic wand, a broom and even cooking utensils.

Building a broomstick, first for sweeping their den, but then found it was good to ride on and big enough for all three

Some items are likely to need sticks of a specific size, and children can be introduced to a simple measuring method without the need for carrying rulers or tape measures. Children should choose sticks of a certain size by using parts of their body, for example, ask the children to find a stick that is the same size as from their elbow to their fingertips and that is three fingers thick. Often children may find items that are too long and so they are shown how to snap the stick to their required size, thus learning another problem solving strategy.

Building large structures

Practitioner preparation

Building larger structures needs some thought on the part of the practitioner. Before embarking on large scale building, consider the following points:

- Is the area used by the general public? If so you will need to dismantle structures at the end of each session, remember "Leave only footprints" message.

- What loose materials are available on your site? Do you need to bring anything extra with your kit, e.g. rope, tarpaulins?

- What types of trees do you have? Is there a variety that can be used?

- Are you able to coppice branches yourself on site or do you need to bring some in?

- Do you offer large construction outdoors within your setting so children to gain the basic skills of building and moving objects safely?

Practitioners' safety points for large scale building

- Do you have safe carrying methods and teach these to your children?

- Do you ensure practitioners have understood the risks and risk benefits associated with the activity?

- Do you practise these safety measures within your setting boundaries, prior to going out further into the environment?

- How do you support children if they use branches or sticks that are clearly rotting and covered with fungus or if they use materials from an area that is a bug or animal home?

- Do you teach your children the message of 'leave only footprints' if you are on a shared or public site?

- Do you allow children to take risks, test their structures, and let them learn about cause and effect, so they can make appropriate adaptations? These are the risk benefits.

- Do you allow children to take risks and challenges within your setting's outdoor area prior to going out further into the environment?

- Do you need to use tools?

■ Do you carry out the correct safety procedure for tool use and follow the Forest School principle that practitioners are trained and qualified for these activities?

Children think about their creations as they build. They utilise a wide range of physical movements as they build and collect. They develop thought processes and negotiating skills as they design, adapt, dismantle, add new areas and then use structures in their play. There is scope for co-operation, communicating with others and taking on board each other's ideas, as well as opportunity for mathematical learning and problem solving.

Practitioners often see different roles being carried out by the children when they are involved in large scale building, ranging from the inventor, the supervisor, the team leader, the builders, the collectors, to those who watch or dip in and out of the activity.

There are also some children who will build on their own with no other help. The need to create their own special space is equally as important as the large communal structures. Children of all ages will find areas to hide away. Some children find the building element of the structure more appealing than the using and playing with it and will equally have gained some important skills. It could be that their social interaction with others for imaginative play needs developing or they simply want to move on to something else if they have spent a great deal of time on the building.

The building process – dens and shelters

When first taking early years' children out to build a den, it is a good idea to place the main ridge of the den securely for the children to discover. This may need lashing (examples are in the appendix to this chapter), or you can securely wedge between branches. You then know that the main support structure is in a firm and safe position to support the weight.

Children should be taught how to carry larger sticks or branches safely. A good guideline to use is: 'Anything that is bigger than you needs another person to help you carry it'. Show children how to position themselves one at each end of the branch.

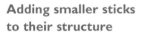

Adding smaller sticks to their structure

Having supplies of natural materials can aid children's den building within their setting

Pegs and materials make a good alternative for den building

Over the course of a year in one Forest School setting, the children soon learnt to build their own independent structures. They will also have learnt through cause and effect, that correct positioning of sticks or branches is crucial for the structure to stay supported.

In settings where there is not much opportunity for using large branches or wood, you may be able to supply some or help children to use covers and tarpaulins in a variety of ways to make shelters. A supply of large pegs is useful as well as some short lengths of rope. Tarpaulins can be bought in a variety of sizes and have holes in many places to allow them to be attached easily to hooks in a wall or suspended between nursery furniture outside.

Other large scale structures

Children will enjoy using logs to make pretend pirate ships, vehicles, dragon dens or traps. When using much larger logs, the use of ropes to pull and drag the logs in place develops the children's teamwork skills and strength. You can even incorporate ancient methods of moving heavy objects as can be found in many history books.

Bridges can lead anywhere

Basic large bridge building for example, might be seen as having limited creativity but this activity challenges children in different ways to solve problems of balance and design. Will it hold their weight? How long does it need to be? These questions will become part of the children's line of enquiry. It may lead adults to supply more information about different styles of bridge building in different parts of the world and at different times in our civilisation.

Children helped build this basic bridge which they could crawl over to their island

This basic bridge also had a rope support

Other large structures

Using loose parts within settings

Building structures on a beach

Some settings may have access to a beach on a regular basis. If this is not the case, try to find out whether any children may be spending their holidays near a beach. A workshop for parents might encourage them to be creative with their children whilst on holiday. Our beaches are rich in treasures that can be used in so many ways. Sticks, pebbles, shells and seaweed can be used to adorn a variety of sand creations. The sand can be used to make castles, pies, forts, a car, a mermaid or a crocodile. There is no end to the list.

Building a large sand fort and waiting for the sea – will it reach it?

If you have a large sandpit in your setting, children may be able to contribute to collections of shells, pebbles and driftwood which can be used in the sandpit. It is a good idea to remove other objects except for buckets and spades. Driftwood and seaweed can be used to build a variety of structures limited only by the creative imaginations of adults and children.

These two girls aged 6 and 4 created a Japanese Sushi restaurant out of natural materials

Conclusion

The building and design of other structures will soon become more creative, as children's imaginations are being sparked in different directions in their play. Adults need to support children's building but not take over or do it for them. As the structures become an integral part of the children's play, children will often have additional ideas about them and by encouraging creativity in this way, play can be extended and developed even further. Adults can encourage the possibility thinking that is discussed in Chapter 2 by asking questions such as: 'Does this den need to be bigger to fit everyone in? Do the children need to add doorways or openings, areas for storage or sleeping? Are there places to store items for cooking or sweeping?'

Some settings may not be able to access plentiful supplies of suitable material. It may be possible to use natural materials in conjunction with the sets of wooden building blocks and planks that are usually found in most settings. Similar rules about helping children build safely will apply, and creativity in design can be furthered by supplying different shaped objects and some natural resources. Acorns and dead leaves have been used as 'moon food' in one setting and carefully stored in the space rocket made of wooden planks and blocks.

There are now many outdoor areas in parks or national trust properties that have areas allocated for building structures. Find out where there are some in your area and encourage families to visit these with their children.

POINTS FOR DISCUSSION

- If you have babies and toddlers could you develop more treasure baskets with natural resources?

- Do you allow babies and toddlers some freedom of movement on different surfaces in the outdoor environment?

- How do you allow children to develop their sustained thinking and creative skills in outdoor structure building in your setting? What could you improve or develop? Think about Anna Craft's 'Possibility thinking'.

- How do you support your children when problems arise when building?

- How often do you seek CPD in creativity and ideas for new large or small structure building ideas?

- Do you experience problems with lack of materials to use? How could you overcome this problem? Do you have access to any local groups to support you? Do you have any parents able to help?

- Reflect upon your Risk Assessments; are they workable?

- Have you looked at a risk benefit for this activity to support evidence of children's risk taking with structure building in outdoors environment? Do you share this evidence with your line managers or head teachers?

- How do you involve your family units with structure building in the outdoors?

USEFUL RESOURCES

The Little Book of Treasure Baskets by Ann Roberts and Sally Featherstone (A. & C. Black, reprint 2012)

Treasure Baskets and Beyond: Realising the Potential of Sensory Rich Play by Sue Gascoyne (Oxford University Press 2012)

Treasure Baskets and Heuristic Play by Sally Featherstone (A & C Black 2013)

Developing Play for the Under 3s: The Treasure Basket and Heuristic Play by Anita Hughes (Routledge 2010)

A Practical Guide to Tying Knots by Geoffrey Budworth (Lorenz Books 2014)

Knots, by Trevor Bounford (Collins Gem 2001)

Websites

www.animatedknots.com

Woking sea rangers – 10 second knots series, YouTube.com

Bibliography

Goddard Blythe, S. (2011) *The Genius of Natural Childhood: Secrets of Thriving Children*. Stroud: Hawthorn.

Appendix

Useful knots to know

There are many useful books, mobile applications, YouTube videos or websites devoted to knot tying, which show you either in picture or video form the correct method. Not everyone is an expert on every single knot known to man; however if you can master just a couple of useful knots to begin with, it will support your own personal practice and structure building with the children. The following knots with example uses are the most useful; once these are mastered you will find others follow similar patterns.

Clove hitch – for starting your lashing, securing

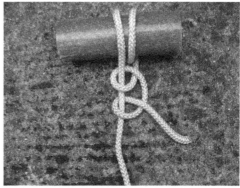

Round turn two half hitches – good for making rope secure

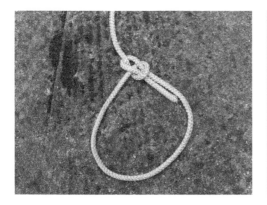

Bowline – secure knot for several purposes

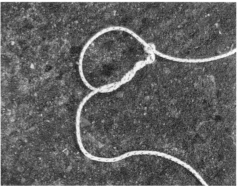

Timber hitch – good for securing – easily adjustable

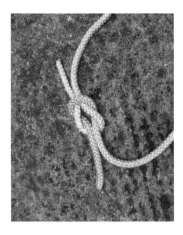

Reef knot – a general purpose knot for securing your rope and can be undone easily

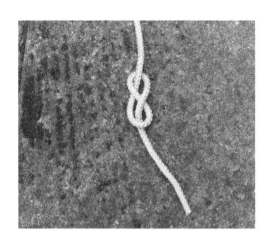

Figure of eight – stopper knot

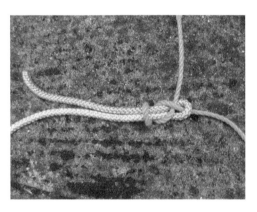

Double sheet bend – for joining two ropes of different thickness together

Lashing square – for securing two pieces of wood together

Eye splice – for a fixed loop, also shows ends sealed

The type of rope used is also important, as there are many types from manmade to natural fibres. Yacht chandleries or outdoor activity stores are a good source for a variety of ropes, twines and information.

- **String** – cotton or natural fibres are best for small construction or models, which will rot down if left out.

- **Natural fibres** – hemp is strong for large construction; however, bear in mind that over time it will rot down and so structures like ladders or supporting branches for dens are likely to collapse over time.

- **Manmade fibres** – there are many types; one, commonly used in Forest School, is Paracord. This is used for many purposes, e.g. supporting hammocks and other structures. It comes in a variety of thicknesses and is fairly strong, but being manmade will not rot down if left in a natural environment.

Examples of thicker rope suitable for early years

Examples of thin twine and paracord for small work

6 Movement outdoors

Parents and practitioners will find many check lists of what children should be doing at the various stages of their early years. In the UK, practitioners refer to the EYFS as their guide to the various stages of development. This chapter explores how the outdoor environment can enhance children's physical development.

The chapter discusses:

■ barefoot activities

■ types of movement from fine motor to gross motor skills

■ movement of babies and toddlers

■ movement involving risk

■ expressive movement outside

■ safety points for practitioners

■ reflective questions.

The environment plays an important role in children's physical development. If they are only exposed to flat asphalt, concrete or safety surfaces, children find it harder to move on uneven terrain. They are also unaware of the risks and take the same approach as if it were a flat surface, only to suffer the consequences.

Children who are regularly exposed to 'wild' outdoor areas will learn skills of balance, observation and spatial awareness to a greater degree. Their knowledge and understanding of the natural environment in its many forms also play a key role. For example, bracken and grasses can change the look of an area during the seasons – in the winter when vegetation has died back, the ground is fairly bare, revealing lumps and dips. During the summer, it will have grown,

Being able to explore in a variety of environment enables children to experience texture, shapes, smell and changes over the seasons

often to a great height, and so the physical clues that the children once saw are no longer there.

Young toddlers need this 'wild' exposure to help them develop and build up their balance and muscle strength. Research has shown that in today's society, children are rarely going barefoot in the outdoors. There could be a variety of reasons, cheapness of shoes, lack of understanding, even health and safety. Podiatrist, Simon J. Wilker explained how walking barefoot is vital in physical development of children, as it supports agility in their feet, ankles, legs, knees and hips. It will support their balance, posture and movement (Wilker 1961). Although his book Take your *Shoes Off and Walk* is out of print, many in the chiropody and occupational therapy field still refer to his research (Hanscom 2014).

With barefoot experiences in mind, there are many activities that you can do outdoors. Create barefoot trails where children walk through or on dry natural objects like bark, pebbles or log circles to then move onto textures like grass, dry soil or compost, and then finish with textures where water has been added, sand or compost which is great for that squelching feeling through the toes and finishing with a warming foot bath full of bubbles. It is interesting to watch the reaction of the children and observe which section is enjoyed the most – the bubble foot bath at the end can be a firm favourite on a warm summer's day.

CASE STUDY: BAREFOOT – NATURAL MUD PIT

A young family was developing part of their long garden into a wild sensory area for the children to use. They had several large log circles and an assortment of smaller cut pieces of wood to make a small circular area. Then, using some lining for the inner circle, they added some compost.

The two children (Lucas, aged 4 years 7 months, and Henry, 18 months) were both helping with the project. Henry was more eager to help and collect the small sticks and materials, while Lucas, who did help with the big logs, was at times more focused on his remote-control toys. With the compost now in place, they were asked if they wanted to see what it felt

Children exploring but the older child prefers to keep his shoes on

Sheer delight for the younger child as he experiences the change to the soil

like in bare feet. Henry had no hesitation in taking his crocks and socks off and got straight into the dry compost pit, wiggling his toes around the mixture. Lucas was very hesitant, saying there were worms and it was dirty. He did eventually go in with his brother, but with his shoes on.

Their mother asked what it might be like if they added some water. Both were eager to help with this job and got their own small watering cans to fill. Henry, still barefoot, was at ease in moving around the whole area of the garden and in the new mud pit. They both poured the water into the pit, Henry pouring from inside, while Lucas chose to sit on a log and pour. Henry was clearly excited by the effect the water was having on the compost, and would squeal with delight, babbling different sounds to express his happiness (no identifiable

Lucas, the older child, is very hesitant about what it will feel like

Adult supports Henry as he attempts to jump, which makes a great splat sound

Henry now has new found interest having experimented with the mud

speech at the moment). After a while Lucas took off his own socks and shoes to try putting his foot in the compost. Very tentatively he managed his toes and quickly took them out again, saying 'that's yucky and cold'. He clearly preferred to remain on the log. Interestingly, he was fine to a certain point with walking around barefoot, provided he was on grass.

Henry's gross motor skills are still developing and he was not quite able to jump off the logs, needing support from an adult at first. However, after a couple of attempts he then tried to jump at first in a half squat position which then changed to a backward crawl off. Then he jumped and landed with both feet, had a little topple and then fell onto his knee. He stood up clearly pleased, making a verbal sound and pointing to his muddy knee.

Henry was then left to explore by himself as his brother had by now lost interest. He continued to stomp around in the mud and then bent down and picked up a handful of mud, which he then threw haphazardly, and it landed with a 'thud' onto one of the logs. Curious, he picked up another handful and a game of splat developed, some landing on the log, others elsewhere. He is clearly showing a level 4 and at times 5 on the Leuven scale as described in Chapter 1.

Henry is clearly bolder in his exploration and not worried by the mud, or different textures being felt under his bare feet. He is also eager to help the adult with building the new area for the garden, but not reached the development stage in which to think of his own designs. He was clearly fascinated by the experience and exploring in a variety of ways, first with the mud dry and then adding water. He was using a variety of gross motor skills within his play which included: climbing, balancing, jumping, squatting, stamping, moulding with his hands, throwing, patting and pouring. He even tried to scoop water that was in the mud back into his watering can to pour again.

It will be interesting to see how the children use this area over time and what other materials or toys they bring to it as they develop their play. Jan White, in her book *Playing and Learning Outdoors*, mentions that if mixing and concocting is provided as a continuous provision, children's development will be extended and their thought process will also be stretched by questions of 'what else could be added?' or 'why did that happen?' (White 2014).

It would also be interesting to observe how Lucas continues to use the area. Will he change his views on the mud? Will he introduce other materials? Will the area remain the same size? This may have been another factor in why Lucas was not as engaged; will he want it to be expanded? Or will it be an area solely used by his brother to explore?

Types of movement

Fine motor movements

The outdoor environment offers opportunities for 'pincer' or fine motor movements as children investigate insects or plants, when they shape the mud or clay, find small twigs that can be snapped for building their small creations, catch the sycamore seeds that twirl down on the breeze of the wind or catch long flowing grass as it gets blown about.

Children of all ages love to collect and gather many natural items like leaves, acorns, fir cones or twigs in a variety of containers or bags of any size, allowing their small hand and finger movements to come into play. Children of all ages enjoy using tools and containers in their play, whether these are scissors for cutting string or grass, spoons of different sizes from very small to giant size, small trowels, forks or small-lidded pots for mixing potions or just digging holes.

Some Forest School settings use other tools, such as peelers or knives for whittling the ends of their sticks in readiness for their marshmallow and then 'fish for the flames' to cook it. A bow saw or billhook for cutting larger

This toddler is fascinated by the flowing grass, and is trying to catch it using his fine motor and hand-eye coordination skills

The smallest things found in nature such as this dandelion offer the most valuable fine motor skills opportunities for a child

This child would find small sticks and he would then hammer into the ground

pieces of wood can also be introduced. Whatever the tool, the initial skills of collecting, moulding, pouring and carrying will all strengthen the child's hands in order for them to acquire the fine motor skills needed for the further tool use and later writing skills.

Gross motor movement

Children will learn and take a variable number of risks as they develop. Children's natural instinct when they first come outside from being indoors is to run. The freedom to run, feel the breeze of the wind, the warmth of the sun or the rain on your face is something that we all remember from our childhoods. Children know what they want their bodies to do and feel. Spinning around or being swung around on the swing for that giddy world flying by feeling, rolling down hills or running down them so fast you feel you can't stop are all experiences that children learn over time and enjoy.

Movement of babies and toddlers

Allowing children different areas of opportunity for them to learn is paramount to their development. Very young children too should be allowed to practise the various stages of physical development and not be hurried along. A baby who has mastered being able to go from a sitting position to a standing position still needs to master the crawling movement. Research has shown that children who crawl are also developing the brain functions required for hand-eye coordination, mental awareness and even learning to take risks. The crawling action causes the child's brain to interact with both sides. Missing out this developmental milestone has shown that some children are showing development delays throughout their childhood (Integrated Learning Strategies 2015). New parents are being encouraged to give their babies 'tummy time' as this all helps to develop the child's muscle strength (Elliott 2006).

Allowing babies tummy time helps strengthen their core muscles and allows their brain to develop new connections for movement

Movement involving risk and sensory experiences

All movement carries some degree of risk, and when children are out in the open environment this risk is increased. We need to look at this as being a 'risk benefit' and the children will be learning from it. If they are always told tree climbing is too dangerous, how will they know if they have been allowed to try for themselves. Many adults and parents feel that they need to protect the child by issuing a verbal warning such as 'Be careful' or offering a quick response such as 'Don't go too high' or 'Mind out! You might fall'. This can have a negative effect on children's confidence. It's very hard as a parent or practitioner to see children taking risks, but if we help them with positive phrases, children will be less reliant upon an adult for help and will manage their risks accordingly. Teacher Tom's blog (http://teachertomsblog.blogspot.co.uk/2015/11/eleven-things-to-say-instead-of-be.html) on 'eleven things to say instead of be careful', gives some useful ideas and phrases to use.

In this photo sequence, a toddler is taking risks with climbing.

Crawling over these logs proves to be hard work. At first this toddler tumbles onto her back, but she is gaining resilience and gets herself back on track to complete the task

This little girl is aged 22 months. She had regular 'tummy time' as a young baby and was a strong crawler. Now she is ready for the next challenge and seems instinctively to know the 'three-point of contact' rule (see below). She was determined to get up onto the first branch of this tree and this was her first tree climbing experience.

Climbing – When learning to climb, start with crawling and balancing activities first for children to gain spatial awareness and posture. Then move to building up the upper body strength and movement. If you have areas within your setting with monkey bars, trapeze bars or rope structures, these will help the child to hold their body weight and move in confined spaces.

Initial stages of learning the three point of contact rule for climbing

This setting has a rope system in place for children to gain strength and balance for when they venture out

When you are outside and there are good climbing opportunities (practitioners need to have checked the tree structure and surrounding areas for any weak or risky areas), guide children to find appropriate handholds and foot placements. Always encourage the 'three points of contact' with early years, this means: two hands and foot, or two feet and one hand on the structure at any one time. Children will go as far as they feel confident. Gradually this will increase with some children, and they will need to learn to assess if the branch is suitable to hold their weight

Another experience for strength, but also to experience what it's like upside down

and that they won't damage the tree. They should also be able to see their way back down, understand how high they are allowed to go, and how many can climb at any one time. You may have some over-confident children, who may need reminding about these messages, as they over-stretch their risk taking. The role of the adult here is to remind and support them if they slip or fall and support their understanding of risk. There are several sources for technical advice and details on the Internet and it is always a good point to check your setting's own policies and insurance.

This child over time has gained confidence to climb, using all the skills mentioned. With the adult nearby he has an understanding of what he is able and allowed to do. The adult too has a good understanding of the child's ability

Running – Being allowed to run free without barriers is something that children aspire to. It offers freedom of expression, speed, co-ordination of the body, spatial awareness and above all fun. If your space is restricted in any way, talk to the children about what they should be aware of before they go out. This will allow them to appreciate that if they want to run – can they stop? Can they avoid any obstacles or people? Will they trip? You will no doubt get the occasional bump or fall as they learn the skill of spatial awareness and control their bodies. Practitioners will need to deal with this in a way that will not deter the child's learning, but equally will make them more aware of what's around them. If a child trips over a small log or long grass, for example, try saying 'Wow are you trying to fly?', rather than rushing over with 'Oh dear, are you ok? Did you hurt yourself?' The latter is likely to bring tears, whilst the former more resilience.

Rolling/sliding/spinning/weaving – Just as with running, rolling, sliding down slopes or spinning or weaving around is a rewarding sensation. Children will experiment, moving their bodies to find new ways of looking at things or enjoying the feeling. Children need to be allowed time to do this. Can you remember the feeling of being upside down as a child or spinning around so much that you fall with dizziness? Being in the open environment will give them the space and freedom to experiment with these movements, observations and feelings.

Many of these fundamental movements need to be experienced in order for the child to process their emotions and experiences around them. Children cannot be expected to mime climbing over a log, twirl like a leaf as it falls, or crawl through long grass, if they have never seen or experienced it first-hand. Many young children merely copy the actions of the adult at first, and might not express their own creativity by thinking about how their body actually moves and what it might feel like.

At Peter Pan Nursery, a group of children were able to work with a movement artist, who was Laban trained, as part of 'Open Sesame', a Creative Project with Surrey, East and West Sussex. She showed the children, by taking them outside to observe first-hand, how leaves fall, and how ivy was twisting around the trees, giving them new language and allowing the children to come up with their own descriptions, a point referred to in Chapter 4. She was also able to observe how the children moved various parts of their body in relation to these sights. Back in the nursery setting she devised some movement games and dances. She then allowed the children to reflect upon their time when outside in the woods and asked them to move like the natural objects that they had observed.

Later during the week, the artist and the children put together a movement dance story, in which the children came up with the ideas of how they can move their bodies to be the objects or settings within the story. Some moved like the water, others floated through the wind, while others stomped and squelched through the mud. The child who played being a puddle was encouraged by a practitioner to follow the other children as they were moving around the room, but he replied that he couldn't because he was the puddle. This child was literally being the puddle, as he was making very small hand movements. Practitioners needed to allow for this within these types of sessions. He was right – puddles don't stand up and walk.

It was interesting to understand ideas from movement theorist Rudolf Laban who developed four component parts for movement, which are: Direction, Weight, Speed and Flow. Within these components there are a further eight efforts of wring, press, flick, dab, glide, float, punch and slash (Espeland 2015).

Children and adults use all these components without thinking. If we observe children when they are sad, angry or excited they will move parts of their body with any one of the above-mentioned components spontaneously and with freedom of expression. Penny Greenland refers to this 'body intelligence' as a means of processing both consciously and unconsciously (Greenland 2000). Quite often we can be seen carrying out particular movements as we perhaps rehearse a situation that we are unsure of before we actually do it.

Freedom of expression with movement outside

We have already talked about the freedom to move creatively in different ways. Most of this movement can then be used outside for a variety of purposes and for children to be able to express their feelings and emotions.

Movement skills needed for:

- Tracking animals: Creeping, crawling, slow movements

- Climbing: Balance, upper body strength, spatial awareness, hand-eye co-ordination, stretching body

- Moving through undergrowth: Bending, crawling, ducking, moving through tight spaces, spatial awareness, balance

- Carrying equipment: Hand-eye co-ordination, strength, spatial awareness, working as a team if the object is large, safety awareness of surroundings

- Using tools: Hand-eye co-ordination, spatial awareness, hand grip, body posture, safety awareness

- Swinging and spinning: Spatial awareness, hand-eye co-ordination, balance, body posture, safety awareness

- Dancing: Free expression, whole body movements, hand-eye co-ordination, balance, body posture, spatial awareness, imagination, emotional feelings

■ Observing nature: Stillness, slow movements, spatial awareness

■ Storytelling: Spatial awareness, general movement around the environment, imaginative movements.

Creating opportunities for movement in other outdoor environments

In a natural open space such as a woodland setting there are many opportunities for children to develop a wide range of movements. However, if you are not able to access such a space on a regular basis then it is important to consider ways of maximising the opportunities for children to move in a variety of creative ways in your setting. This may go back to the basic design and layout of your outdoor space and may necessitate some creative thinking on the part of the adults. Some settings still have fixed climbing apparatus such as a frame or slide which occupies quite a lot of space but may not allow children to be particularly creative in the way they use it. Sometimes it can be adapted with the addition of planks for balancing and sliding or hammocks for swinging.

Setting up a hammock can be a fairly easy process for any setting, and it does not need to have trees. Weight bearing posts, or strong hooks are a good alternative

If possible some tree branches or logs can be a useful addition to any space. A local tree surgeon may be able to help with this. Small logs can be moved around by the children as they wish and large ones can be used for balancing. Large cable drums too can be sourced as another resource to challenge children's larger physical movements. Adults can often encourage children to think about the way they are moving on these resources and they may challenge them to move in different ways across a series of obstacles. Fine motor skills can be developed as mentioned above, as children pick up and work with small natural objects such as grasses, nuts, acorns, small twigs, conkers, pebbles and rocks. Mention has been made in several chapters of the importance and benefits of providing a rich collection of natural resources.

A woodwork bench offers opportunity for using tools

A selection of soft wood offcuts and maybe some fabrics, ribbons and natural resources will enable children to use their creative skills as they use these in conjunction with real tools.

Conclusion

When we consider movement, be it for a purpose or creatively, it needs to be nurtured from the beginning. We have seen how missing various stages of movement can lead to some delay in other areas of the child's development, as mentioned with regard to crawling. We have mentioned too that children who only experience flat surfaces in built-up areas and who are not able to experience open areas find it difficult to deal with the unpredictable ground in woodland or field, for example. Practitioners therefore need to be creative in these situations to provide children with a variety of areas for children to develop spatial awareness, resilience and strength, enabling them to develop their full potential.

Getting children outside shows clear benefits for their physical health and wellbeing and going out on a regular basis, as with a Forest School session, allows children to repeat and develop their physical skills over time. As Sara Knight mentions 'being outside and enabling children to engage with their environment also encourages habits of exercise that can be sustained' (Knight 2013).

This child is learning to take risks within her setting. She first tests her idea; once satisfied, she cautiously takes the challenge

We see how the Forest School ethos allows for children to take and manage their own risks. Not every child will want to climb a tree, but learning to balance along a fallen trunk is equally as valuable. We see, too, how the natural world can offer ideas for children's creative movement and dance.

Finally, we see how the natural world can offer children and adults a place for silence and stillness: a place for thinking, a place for watching and a place for appreciating the smallest thing.

PRACTITIONER SAFETY POINTS

- Risk assess any tree climbing areas

- Check policies and insurance for tree climbing

- Have regular site checks, note and remove any hazards

- Observe spaces for running activities/games, note any hazards

- Carry out a site check for barefoot activities

- Ensure your tools are maintained after each use

- Check your first aid kits and burns kit if using fire

POINTS FOR DISCUSSION

- Can you give opportunities for climbing?

- If you are unable to offer climbing opportunities, can you offer areas outdoors for balancing?

- Can you create opportunities for expressive movement outside?

- Do you have any areas where stillness and quiet can be observed?

- Can you offer barefoot activities?

USEFUL RESOURCES

http://www.forestschoolassociation

http://www.cultureshift.org.uk/what-we-do/open-sesame/

http://www.kidsafensw.org/imagesDB/wysiwyg/TreeClimbing2015_5.pdf

http://creativestarlearning.co.uk/early-years-outdoors/big-rope-play/

https://www.ltl.org.uk/spaces

Sharing Nature with Children by Joseph Cornell (DAWN Publications 1998)

Animals: Tracks, Trails and Signs by R.W. Brown, M.J. Lawrence and J. Pope (Octopus Publishing Ltd 1992)

101 Games for Social Skills by Jenny Mosley and Helen Sonnet (LDA 2003)

Let's Go Outside by Steph Scott and Katie Akers (Batsford 2015)

Run Wild! Outdoor Games and Adventures by Fiona Danks and Jo Schofield (Frances Lincoln Ltd 2011)

The Wild City Book by Jo Scofield and Fiona Danks (Frances Lincoln Ltd 2014)

Nature's Playground by Fiona Danks and Jo Schofield (Frances Lincoln Ltd 2005)

Giraffes Can't Dance by Giles Andrede and Guy Parker-Rees (Orchard Books 2015)

Friends Together by Rob Lewis (Red Fox 2000)

The Midnight Gang by Margaret Wild and Ann James (Southwood Books 1996)

Bibliography

Elliott, J. (2006) 'Babies need "tummy time" to develop'. Retrieved from BBC News, 1 July: http://news.bbc.co.uk/1/hi/health/5128144.stm.

Espeland, T. (2015) 'The eight efforts: Laban Movement'. Retrieved from Theatrefolk, 23 March: https://www.theatrefolk.com/blog/the-eight-efforts-laban-movement/.

Greenland, P. (2000) *Hopping Home Backwards*. Manningtree: Jabadao.

Hanscom, A. J. (2014) *Balanced and Barefoot*. Oakland, CA: New Harbinger.

Integrated Learning Strategies (2015) 'The learning risks when babies skip the crawling phase'. Retrieved from ILS Learning Corner, 8 February: https://ilslearningcorner.com/why-babies-should-never-skip-the-crawling-phase/.

Knight, Sara (2013) *Forest School and Outdoor Learning in the Early Years* (2nd edition). London: Sage.

White, J. (2014) *Playing and Learning Outdoors*. London: Routledge.

Wilker, S. (1961) *Take off your Shoes and Walk*, 1st edition. New York: Devon-Adair Co.

7 Colour, shape, pattern and form in the natural world

In this chapter, we discuss some of the colours, shapes, patterns and forms found in the natural world. Artists have been taking inspiration from the natural world since prehistoric times. Cave paintings over 30,000 years old show how human beings were able to use the natural materials around them to depict some of the creatures and plants in their world.

Some well-known artists of today are still using similar materials, the earth itself, its soils and stones or parts of plants and trees to create their works of art. Examples are given later in the chapter. Many other artists through the ages have been inspired by the natural landscape and the world of nature, with its complexities of myriads of natural shapes, patterns and colours.

We will look at:

■ ways we can encourage children to use a variety of materials and to be able to make their own creations in an outdoor space

■ the three main stages in this process:

• exploration

• observation

• inspiration

■ ideas for you and your children to discover in these three categories

■ provision of a wide range of resources.

Exploration

Young babies need to explore and can benefit from access to an imaginative variety of different objects. The main point to remember is that they use their mouths to explore, so resources need to be carefully chosen. Careful supervision is crucial but babies can explore many different textures and shapes without coming to harm.

This photo shows the baby on the beach, but it is easy to provide collections of beach objects for babies to explore, large pebbles of different shapes and textures, seaweed, shells, pieces of driftwood (check for any splintered edges but often this wood is smooth).

Think too about offering treasure baskets with resources made from natural materials. Wooden objects can often be found in the kitchen, spoons of different shapes and sizes, a spirtle and a spatula. Small rollers suitable for massage are great for babies to explore as they have moving parts. As they develop more hand control, you can offer different items such a large shiny leaves or pine cones. A mirror made from safety glass can be used to reflect these items or even the clouds in the sky or a moving branch.

As babies start to move they need to experience different textures as they crawl and then walk. Soft mosses, wavy grasses, bracken or crunchy leaves are just a few of the materials they can discover safely.

Discuss the colours and textures of these as the children explore with their senses. Sand, water and clay are essential natural materials for children to explore and they can be encouraged to make marks, shapes and patterns as they play.

Exploring a piece of seaweed

Everyday objects can be placed in a treasure basket for babies to explore

Babies love to explore different textures

Mixing potions – younger children enjoy larger scale mixing and older children develop enough coordination to use a pestle and mortar

Going for a walk is an exciting prospect for young children. As soon as they can walk a few steps, they should be encouraged to walk in different places – on a beach, through rough grass, fields and woods, if possible. Parks offer different surfaces and places to explore whether with a family or a group from nursery. Young children need time to explore at their own pace. As they become more confident they will explore their surroundings in more depth and enjoy a sense of adventure and freedom. With encouragement they will begin to experiment, mixing water with sand or soil to make 'pies' or 'cakes'. Water can be mixed with a variety of different soils and berries to make different shades to paint with. Offer sticks and brushes, charcoal and chalk. Children at one nursery use a pestle and mortar to grind chalk, charcoal and other natural materials when paint making. Using a grater is also another way to break down solid items. In settings where these natural items are not freely available

you can make natural paint from a variety of fruit and vegetables, grating carrot or red cabbage can produce an interesting mix. Opening a pomegranate will promote curiosity and some new vocabulary as children discover the red seeds inside.

Observation – colour

Hold babies so they can observe the different shapes and colours of leaves

Babies will observe what is going on around them as part of their exploration of the world and can be shown different shapes and colours, but as children get older they can be encouraged to look at things more closely for themselves.

Allowing children to observe the outdoors in all weathers will enable them to see the different tones and shades made by the sunlight, rain and snow. A supply of lenses of different sorts should be easily accessible and there are many special containers for observing small creatures. Children enjoy using binoculars too, although this is a difficult skill to learn. They also enjoy looking through coloured film, even lenses that change the perspective or recreate an insect's vision. Making, filling and hanging birdfeeders should encourage a range of birds to visit for children to observe. Encourage children to look at leaves, plants and bark and talk about the textures and patterns you see. Mirrors placed under trees give a different perspective for children to observe. This activity can be extended by using photographs and pictures. Provide cameras for children to use.

Use the language of colour as you talk to the children. Talk about shades and whether they vary from pale to dark. Many colours have a range of words you can introduce. Navy, turquoise, magenta, crimson, lemon, viridian, etc., will encourage children to observe and discriminate colours more accurately. Look at different shades of green when you go outdoors. Talk about the colours of plants and vegetables they may be growing. In one Reggio Emilia preschool children were drawing sunflowers inspired by the famous van Gogh painting. They work in an area of their setting called an atelier, which is set out like an art studio. On the resource shelf was a whole range of well sharpened coloured pencils in many shades of yellow and green. Children selected which ones they wanted to use to create their sunflower. Look closely at flower petals and the way some of them show different colours even on the same plant according to the stage of growth. Autumn leaves or flower petals from a bouquet or from the ground can be collected by children in any setting and can be used in a whole range of different activities. Children can use them as they wish to add to collections, use with sand or water play, collage, and painting.

Collect feathers and looks at the colours. Is it possible to identify the bird by the colour of the feather? It is possible now to buy natural coloured feathers but it is much more exciting for a child if they can discover them for themselves.

Observation – shape, pattern and form

Children will begin to notice shapes as they observe the world around them. Some will be found in manmade materials such as bricks and tiles, but there are many shapes to be observed in the world of nature. Trees are generally recognised by the shape of their leaves and children will enjoy making a leaf collection.

The use of pattern in the natural world is complex and varied. Many artists have taken inspiration from these. Tree bark, vines that twist, fungi, mosses and lichen all give beautiful patterns and shapes. Encourage children to look up at the clouds and using imagination get them to see shapes and objects within them; even the vapour trails from aeroplanes create patterns in the sky.

Butterflies and moths demonstrate mirror or bilateral symmetry in their shape and patterns. Children can use mirrors to find the line of symmetry on a leaf for example. A starfish is an example of radial symmetry and a flower is an example of rotational symmetry.

Going on a walk in woodland can create an opportunity for children to look for examples of symmetry. Some things they will be able to collect and examine in more depth later, but a camera is useful for taking pictures of other large objects such as the end of a fallen tree trunk. Once the photos are printed out, children can use mirrors to observe the patterns and discuss their findings.

Complex patterns are found in many features such as this log

Spirals are common and children usually spot these in snail shells but they can be found in plants too. A collection of pine cones shows how repeated patterns are used in different ways to create different cones. Animal markings provide many different patterns and close observation of the feathers on the back of a duck can provide inspiration.

Stripes and spots can be found on many different creatures and children will enjoy discovering these either through first-hand experience or looking at photographs in a reference book.

Patterns can also be found by observing the movement of light on water or on a field of grass. Children can make patterns on water in a water play area, using different objects to blow through or swirl it around, and the addition of some colour often makes this a popular activity.

Outdoors, water found in puddles or a pond can be moved by using sticks or long soft willow stems to swirl the water.

Children love creating ripples and observing the movement of the water

Children are often drawn to throwing objects into water to see the ripple effect. Care is needed here to ensure that throwing is done safely and also it will not harm any creatures which may be living in the water.

Inspiration

The adults who are with the children on a day to day basis are the first inspiration. Work alongside the children as they make their own creations using natural materials. You may give them ideas for their own work but it is important to remember to encourage them to use their own ideas, not just to copy what you are doing.

Working with leaves

Alex (2 years 5 months) has been going to Forest School from an early age. She watched an adult make a frame for a leaf pattern using sticks and then decided she would do the same. She arranged her leaves carefully and was able to name the colours yellow and green. She then selected twigs, small ones at first, and made a basic square. She then used slightly thicker ones and made a triangle shape. The adult handed her another one saying, 'That's a big one'. She repeated the words, 'big one', and carefully laid it on the other side of the frame. Amelia (aged 2) had been observing Alex and then decided to help her by picking up sticks and leaves and handing them to Alex for the pattern.

During this activity Alex demonstrated a particularly high level of involvement and concentration on her task seen in the following pictures.

Exciting resources can be the source of inspiration for many of the children's artistic creations. You may be able to use the natural resources that are lying around on a beach or in a wood, but any setting can provide collections of natural objects for children to use as they wish. Leaves can be the source of inspiration for many activities, either in a forest setting or a smaller outdoor space. Children will use them in so many different ways.

Jack selected leaves of a certain shape and colour and started to lay them end to end. He became more involved as his line got longer and he worked at this activity for around fifteen minutes. Other children became interested and loved walking alongside the line when he had finished

Inspiration will come from the resources themselves but there are many other ways to inspire children. Good quality reference books and internet photographs can be used to show how professional artists work in the outdoor environment. Sculpture parks make an exciting place to take children. Many sculptures are inspired by the natural world. There are usually animal sculptures, abstract forms inspired by nature and sculptures made from natural materials.

Taking children to a sculpture park offers a wide variety of shapes and forms for them to observe

Children on a school outing to Wisley gardens were asked to look at sculptures in the garden and then go out to collect natural materials and create their own sculpture in a special area outside.

Children from Randolph Beresford Early Years centre go to Wimbledon Common once a week for 'Big Forest School'. One week the group came across artists painting the landscape. The next week staff took appropriate resources and the children were able to talk to the artists and then create their own work. The theme was also developed over time in their 'Little Forest School' back in their own setting. Children showed awareness of colours and shapes and their work was displayed in the setting. They also mixed their own paints using mud and soil.

These photos show the way an interest was extended over time as staff provided appropriate resources and then displayed the children's work

**Working outdoors
on the common**

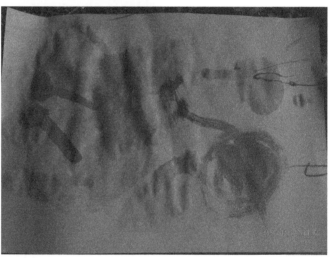

**Back in the
setting**

The final display of the children's artwork

Andy Goldsworthy made an installation in 2013 using coloured leaves around the base of a tree giving the effect of a luminescent glow. Pictures of many of his works can be found online. He uses sticks, pebbles, flower petals and leaves to create shapes and patterns in and around other natural objects such as trees or rocks. Photographs of some of these may give children confidence to work on a larger scale. A woodland offers space for creations on a large scale and it may not be possible to do this in smaller outdoor spaces. However, try occasionally to make somewhere special for children to work with natural objects and ideally leave the work for others to see or for them to revisit at a later time. If space is limited, another way to display the children's work is for them to build it into hanging mobiles. This may require the use of paper as a background or objects may be threaded and hung at different heights.

Children enjoy mixing water and soil and, as mentioned earlier, can make different shades to use as paint. Adults can encourage this and also offer additional inspiration by providing pictures of the work of some of the soil artists working today. Yusuke Asai is a self-taught artist working in Japan. He uses soil, dirt, cow dung and straw to create large scale murals. He collects soil samples from the geographical area that he is working in, grinds them into fine powder and mixes it with water to make paint.

Children at Peter Pan nursery sometimes use pewter in a number of their creative projects at Forest School. One child, whose granddad is a blacksmith, could not contain his excitement when he learnt he was going to melt some metal during his Forest School session. He needed to make a clay mould. He chose a Y shaped stick and pressed it into the clay to make his mould. The adult poured the molten pewter into the mould and it needed to cool for five minutes. He commented on the fact that the pewter had changed from a solid to a liquid and it was 'all wibbly wobbly like my milk'.

Pewter can be melted for children to use to make sculptures

Lighting a fire and sitting round it is now a popular activity with many settings even if there is no access to a woodland. The colour of the flames can be changed by adding sachets of specially produced chemical products known as 'mystical fire'. These are different objects including pine cones which have been specially coated to produce blues and greens in the flames. Once the fire has died down and is really cold, ash and charcoal can be collected from the fire and will provide children with another resource to experiment with. In the cave paintings of Lascaux, shades of red and yellow have been created from the ground to create pictures and another technique used by cave artists was to place a hand on a rock and spray the paint around it to leave an imprint. This is something which children today still enjoy and they could use paint made from soil.

The fire itself can change materials which children can use for sculpting. Pewter is one example. Pewter sticks or powder can be purchased from craft stores or online. Watching the solid form change into a liquid offers a rich learning opportunity for the children. Care must be observed when melting pewter. Adults should use safety gloves. A cuttlefish bone can also make a good mould. Children can use a sharp implement to scratch out a shape or pattern.

The seasons themselves are a great source of inspiration for many artists and children can be supported in their observations of seasonal changes through the year. Materials can be used in different ways. In winter there may be access to ice and snow, and children respond well to using shades of white and grey to create snowy pictures.

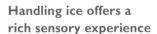

**Handling ice offers a
rich sensory experience**

In spring, the natural awakening of plants and trees encourages us to look at the fresh shades of green, the brightness of spring bulbs, yellow daffodils and brightly coloured tulips. Summer brings its own experiences of colours as children may visit a beach or play in sunlit woods. Autumn brings fresh collections of conkers and acorns for children to use, fallen leaves and twigs and a rich range of colours and shades. Many settings encourage activities such as leaf printing in the autumn. Encourage children to look closely at the shade of paint you offer and support them as they to learn to mix their own colours. Offer fine good quality brushes to encourage them to recreate fine details. A bird's feather can also be used to trail patterns.

Provision of resources

Children at Peter Pan had been listening to the story Mother Earth (see appendix Chapter 4).

At the end of the story each child was given a small piece of clay and encouraged to find natural resources around in the forest which they could use to build a creature as in the story. Children were able to combine their physical skills of dexterity, observational skills and their imagination to produce their creature. The creatures were named and placed on the trunks of nearby trees so everyone could see them.

Children enjoyed making creatures with clay and natural materials following the Mama Earth story (see appendix to Chapter 4)

Similarly the provision of natural resources to enhance play with sand and water can extend and deepen children's involvement. Sand cakes, pies and tarts can be decorated with petals, moss, acorns, etc. It may be possible to take photographs and create a 'recipe book' to share with parents and friends.

A supply of well-maintained resources that children can access themselves needs to be provided. It should include a wide range of natural materials and also a range of materials for mark making. Children may want to use paper or a special place on the ground to work with their ideas. They need to be able to share these ideas with the adults if they wish, or they may prefer to work quietly on their own. Sometimes a child will begin a creation as in the leaf work case study and other children become interested and then may join in. Peer recognition is as important as adult recognition.

Conclusion

The natural world is the greatest resource we have for inspiration. It is the source of colour and shapes. Intricate patterns are seen in the plants and the creatures around the world. Markings help us to distinguish species. Artists are inspired by the patterns on a bird's wing or the moving colours as sunlight passes over fields and hills. Children too will be inspired if we share our excitement and interest in the things around us. By observing closely, we too will become more involved with the beauty that surrounds us. We need to talk to children about our discoveries and make time to observe and listen to the children as they too make discoveries.

One of the best ways to encourage children is to talk about what they have done but instead of asking 'What's that?' try to ask them to talk about what they are doing and share some of their thoughts. If they sense that you value what they are doing they will become more confident and more creative. Children need to feel that there is time for them to work on something; a special place where they can leave things they create over a period of time is also helpful. This may not always be possible, but there may be ways of preserving children's work and ideas maybe through photographs, or making them into hanging decorations which take up less floor space.

Valuing children's creations will enhance their creativity and you can offer inspiration too as you maybe work alongside them, or share the work of artists. Some of the more expensive art books can be borrowed from libraries and children may enjoy looking with you at some of the websites suggested. Open

Hanging decorations are a good way to display children's creations if there is not much floor space

your eyes and mind to what is around and you will be able to share your experiences and encourage children's natural inborn creativity.

POINTS FOR DISCUSSION

■ What resources do you have for children to use to design and create patterns and shapes outdoors? Are you able to add to these resources and if so how? Think about using parents and other adults in the community to help you.

■ If you do not have access to woodland is there anywhere in your setting where you can create spaces for children to leave their installations or creations made from different materials?

■ Can you provide a variety of ways for children to draw and paint outdoors using different materials and methods?

■ Are your resources well maintained, offering a wide range of choice and easily accessible to children?

■ How do you encourage children to look closely at colours and patterns in the natural world? Can you inspire them further by offering cameras, photographs and maybe even a visit from an environmental artist?

USEFUL RESOURCES

The Little Book of Treasure Baskets (Featherstone Education Ltd 2002)

Collaboration with Nature by Andy Goldsworthy (Abrams 1998)

Ephemeral Works 2004–2014 by Andy Goldsworthy (Abrams Books 2015)

Wood by Andy Goldsworthy and Terry Friedman (Thames and Hudson 2010)

Natural: Land Art through the Seasons by Marc Pouyet (Frances Lincoln 2009)

What is Symmetry in Nature? (Looking at Nature) by Bobbie Kalman (Crabtree Publishing 2010)

Seeing Symmetry by Lorren Leedy (Holiday House reprint edition 2013)

Is It Symmetrical? (Little world math concepts) by Nancy Allen (Rourke Publishing Group 2010)

Patterns – The Art, Soul, and Science of Beholding Nature – Patterns in Nature, an online book – Nature's web of life: www.patternsinnature.org/Book/PatternsContain Symmetry.html

Art Forms in Nature by Ernst Haeckel (Dover 1974)

Land Art by Richard Shilling: www.richardshilling.co.uk

Leaf Man by Lois Ehlert (Harcourt Children's Books 2005

Red Leaf Yellow Leaf by Lois Ehlert (Harcourt Publishers' Group 1991)

Both these books will inspire and excite children to look closely at the colours of autumn leaves.

8 Music and sound outdoors

This chapter examines the importance of music in our everyday lives and focuses in particular on ways of encouraging music making outdoors. It stresses the importance of building music into daily life with children rather than just using it as time filler at the end of a session. This chapter encourages us to develop our own listening skills as well as those of children by sharing listening experiences together.

Case studies illustrate how children use materials creatively to make music of different kinds, and there is analysis of the skills children are acquiring through these experiences. The chapter ends with suggestions for adults to reflect on their own practice.

The chapter offers ideas and information on:

■ our musical inheritance and its role in society

■ the importance of learning to listen and ways to enhance listening skills in different environments outdoors

■ ideas on making sound patterns and a variety of instruments from natural materials

■ experimenting with sound making with different objects

■ using music to develop imagination through dance, movement or storytelling

■ using our voices.

Music through the ages

Music has played an important role in human culture from a very early age. In 2012 a team of scientists discovered flutes made from bird bone and mammoth ivory in a cave in Germany. Carbon dating has shown that they are 43,000 years old. The team felt that music played a role in the maintenance of larger social networks and this in turn helped our species expand their territory at the expense of the more conservative Neanderthals.

Music still plays an integral part in all societies today. People practise their own songs, play their own instruments and there is a huge range of musical styles across the world. Most of us will hear music played somewhere every day. It is used in shops as a background, on television and radio and accompanies videos and films. Small children are exposed to a wide variety of musical sounds even before they are born.

Research has been done to examine the ways in which young children respond to music and evidence has been offered to suggest that children who hear music from an early age develop skills which help them decode and learn spoken language earlier.

Peery et al. (1987) suggest that children should be exposed to music and it should be offered in early childhood to ensure a comprehensive learning experience. Memory tasks such as learning times tables can often be made easier by speaking rhythmically, tapping out time or singing the words. Children with highly developed musical intelligence recognise tonal and rhythmic patterns but are also able to understand the relationship between sound and feeling.

This emotional connection between sound and feeling is one of the main reasons why music is so important to us all and it can induce a whole variety of emotional responses by the use of different combinations of tone, volume, tempo and pitch and a variety of different instruments. Musical sounds in the natural world have been recognised as having an important part to play in our society. Scientists have recorded the songs of whales and discovered that their overall song structure uses musical intervals between notes that are similar to the intervals in ours (Hartshorne 1973).

Studies of birdsong have also revealed the complexity of musical themes of many species. An examination of bird song reveals every elementary effect found in human music. There are key changes, harmonic relations and retention of melody. Some birds pitch their songs to the same scale as in western music (Armstrong 1963).

In 2016, BBC Radio 3 played music where instrumentalists and vocalists worked outside and made recordings to include birdsong as well as their own music. Just listening to a few minutes of birdsong on the radio enables one to be transported into fresh woodland, see the sunlight filtering through the trees and smell the damp moss. This experience however is dependent on having had first-hand experience of being in the woods and then being able to recreate it through imagination. Much of our imaginative thinking is based on real experience and our minds can then go on to create fantasy worlds. By giving children real first-hand experiences, we will help them to develop their imaginations and music can play an important part in this.

Listening – an important contributor to creativity

Rachel didn't move. Even though she heard her mother calling her she could hear other things too. There was the whisper of the tall grass and knotweed she stood knee deep in: the twitterings of sparrows settling down for the evening: the laughing cry of a robin as it flew off a fence post. She could even hear the tiny rustlings of small creatures, field mice and shrews – running along tunnels in the grass.

Rachel went on to become one of the most creative scientists of her time, but from the time she was very young she felt a bond with nature. She spent much of her time dreaming about oceans and listening to the sound of crickets. Her work as an adult scientist to ban harmful chemicals has helped to assure that future generations too will be able to dream about oceans and listen to crickets.

Listening to Crickets: A Story about Rachel Carson by Candice Ransom

Learning to listen

'*Listening is the key to learning and learning is a lifelong process which keeps us stimulated and engaged*' (www.creativelisteningcenter.com).

Listening is a skill which needs to be learnt as opposed to our ability to hear, which is innate unless we are born with an auditory problem. Young babies quickly become attuned to a variety of loud sounds, often accompanied by flashing lights, as they experiment with one of the plastic toys so popular and commonly available. The child's senses begin to associate these sounds with the lights and hand movement rather than listening to the sound itself. Nature presents us with a whole range of alternatives. Young babies can be taken outside and just held quietly under a tree where the breeze is blowing. They can hear and often will begin to listen for longer periods to the sounds of rustling leaves. Babies can be placed outside in their sleeping cots or prams, and if possible, placed where they can watch the moving branches of trees, hear the rustle of leaves or swaying grass. An older toddler can walk through autumn leaves and with the help of a supporting adult become aware of the different sounds that can be made according to the way his feet move.

In the book, *The Listening Book: Discovering your own Music*, Mathieu describes the way in which the power of listening becomes an instrument of self-discovery and personal transformation. He suggests that by exploring our capacity for listening to sounds and making music we can awaken and release our full creative powers.

Listening into the distance is like looking into the horizon. When we gaze at the horizon our vision goes beyond our eyes and sees forever. When we listen into the distance our ears reach beyond the farthest sounds and the infinite becomes sensible.

(Mathieu 2011, p. 6)

Listening to the sounds around

Raising awareness

It is important that adults become aware of the sounds around them and are able to stand with the children and tune in to what can be heard. Before you take children outdoors, go outside and make time to tune in to the sounds around. In an urban space you may only initially be aware of traffic or aircraft noise, but in time you will also begin to hear other sounds: footsteps, birdsong, falling leaves, or raindrops. In a woodland space on a still day, you may become aware too of the silence itself, broken only by the snapping of a twig or a distant bird or animal call.

This group of boys have been encouraged to listen and describe the sounds they hear when holding a large sea shell to their ears

In the woods

At Bus Stop Nursery children were playing outside when a sudden strong gust of wind blew through the trees and rustled the leaves. The adult immediately responded and drew the children's attention to this. 'Can you hear the leaves in the wind? What sort of sounds are they making?'

Child: 'Whooshing and swishing.'

The group listened attentively. Another child said, 'I can hear a snail.' Another one replied, 'I can hear a worm'. They all continued to listen for a short time before resuming their play.

Listening to the sound of the wind at Bus Stop Nursery

Children at Peter Pan are encouraged to listen to the song of the robin before they enter the woods. They stand with their leader and wait quietly until birdsong is heard or if this doesn't happen they may hear another natural sound instead. Once children are in the woods they are encouraged to listen to the sounds around them. If it is damp or raining they hear water dripping through the trees or making a beat on the tarpaulin. They hear the splash as they run through puddles or the crunch of a twig as they step on it.

In the town

In an urban environment, there may be the nearby sounds of children playing, or traffic on the street. Further listening will encourage children to pick out different sounds, e.g. laughter, a car horn, a motor bike roaring. In many settings, it may be possible to hear aircraft overhead and this may range from far off planes to those heard nearer an airport.

However, there are always natural sounds to be heard in amongst the noise of an urban space. There will be birds, and often there are trees and leaves. A garden space in a setting will offer a rich habitat for wildlife. It may be possible to hear frogs croaking, bees humming and maybe the sounds of water trickling in a pond or water feature. Can you hear a bird singing? Encourage birds into your urban space by hanging bird feeders or providing nesting material or a bird box. Encourage children to listen to the songs and sounds made by different birds. There are Internet sites, CDs and books available if you need help with this and wish to identify the sounds of different species (see resource list at the end of this chapter).

In the local park

Many settings in urban environments may be able to use their local park. There will be the sounds of children playing, dogs barking or nearby traffic but try to become aware of other sounds, e.g. leaves moving on the trees, birdsong or small creatures moving in undergrowth. Different seasons of the year offer different listening experiences.

On a beach

Some practitioners are able to take children on the beach and there are an increasing number of beach schools in this country. The sounds of the seaside may be familiar to us all but as you listen to the sound of waves, it is possible to break the sound down into different 'tunes'. There are short bursts of light sounds, the swish on the sand as a wave breaks and the sound of pebbles being pulled back on an ebbing wave. On a stormy day there is a constant roar in the background as each wave crashes in a steady surge. These can be recreated in other environments by the use of 'ocean drums'. (See resource list.)

Seagulls flying, dogs barking, all contribute to the sound patterns of the beach. Pebbles and rocks can be used to make sounds too as they strike one against the other or are thrown into the sea.

Listening to sounds made by the weather

Seize the opportunity to go outside on a windy day. Listen to the sounds. Are they different? How can you describe the wind? Can you make a sound like the wind? Offer children some metal, plastic or bamboo tubes or pipes and let them experiment outside with wind propelled sound. If high winds are predicted it is safer not to go out.

Snowfall has a magical effect on sounds as it muffles everyday sounds. Snow itself can creak, squeak and crack as you walk on it. This muffled stillness all around you, allows to you to focus on your own sounds of breathing and heart beats. Children can thus become aware of their own body sounds.

Rain creates a myriad of sound patterns depending on its strength and where it is falling. Rain on a tin roof is very different from a plastic roof, water dripping slowly from gutters or rushing out as a surge if gutters are blocked. Young children love playing with and collecting rain.

Making a map of sounds

Once children have understood that they can make marks to represent objects they might enjoy making a musical sound map. As they get older, their marks will become more representative of the sounds they hear and maybe the source of the sound. Younger children may be able to do this activity using natural materials. They will be gaining some understanding of spatial awareness and auditory discrimination as they record relative distances and directions of sounds. Provide a large sheet of paper. Children mark themselves in the centre and then record the sounds they hear in the approximate direction of the sound with some clue as to the nature of what is making the sound. They can share these experiences with a friend or an adult. This activity can be done using just natural objects; get the children to collect many natural objects – sticks, pebbles, feathers etc. and as before get them to stand in an area and place their objects one at a time and in the direction of the sound they hear.

Making sound patterns using natural materials

Rocks, pebbles, sticks, cones, acorns, conkers and moss are just some of the natural materials that can be found and collected to offer a range of pattern making experience. Children will begin to experiment on their own, but it may require sensitive adult intervention and support to encourage them to develop their initial responses to create something more sustained. In one urban nursery a selection of pebbles, wood, shells and cones was placed on a table. A. used a selection of stones and built himself a xylophone. He then chose two wooden sticks and used them to play his small instrument listening to the variety of sounds made by the pebbles. An adult was supporting this activity by her presence at the table but the idea came from the child and he was able to follow out his ideas (see Case Study, Chapter 9).

Using sticks with different natural objects creates many different sounds

Using sticks to make music and sounds

Sticks are the most obvious material to use to make sound patterns and the two case studies show how individual children can use them in different ways.

CASE STUDY: ON A FAMILY WALK

From a very young age, Harry has always liked a stick. At the age of two he would use a stick to explore muddy puddles or simply to poke around on the ground. Now on a family walk, a stick is an essential part of his equipment. He chooses a stick carefully and if it breaks, he can get very upset. He then likes to find another one that meets with his approval. One day he was asked to see how many sounds he could make with this stick. He became very involved and started to experiment with his stick on different types of trees. He discovered that different trees made different sounds when they were tapped, and also he could make softer sounds if he used his stick more gently. He began to beat out different rhythm patterns and moved his body in time with his 'stick song' as he called it.

We asked him to listen as we walked through the woods and tell us what other sounds he could discover. The ground was covered in fallen leaves and he used his stick to swish them around and his feet to make a variety of sounds. When walking quickly through the leaves in a steady rhythmic way, he said it sounded like a train.

The role of the adult was supportive and encouraged Harry to begin to experiment rather than just walk along swinging his stick and not engaging with his surroundings in any depth. Now, when he goes out, he often initiates something similar for his own enjoyment.

CASE STUDY IN FOREST SCHOOL: 'LET THERE BE DRUMS'

During Forest School sessions, we found many occasions to make and listen to different sounds by picking up sticks of all different shapes and sizes and finding different surfaces to hit them. Initially this was introduced as a group activity, where children would each find their own stick about an arm's length and then choose their own tree to tap against it. Over the following weeks the children became familiar with the activity and some would look more carefully for a special stick, where initially they had just picked up the closest one, regardless of its size or

Many children in Forest School at Peter Pan enjoy creating drums

state of decay. This repeated activity had enabled the children to learn that some of their sticks broke easily, were difficult to hold or that the thickness would make a different sound. They also learnt that the surface they chose to strike upon would also have an impact upon the sound.

One particular child (C.) was fascinated by this activity and his first action when outside was to find something that he could use to hit 'his drums'. There are a number of small log stumps that the children use. C. had moved a few of these closer together so he could use them as drums. He had found two different types of sticks, one thick and one thin, which he used one at a time on his 'drums'.

C. developed his play from first experimenting with the materials and the sounds, to using materials and sounds with a purpose. He had the freedom to move from place to place to explore how the sounds are different on different surfaces.

Initially his activity was fairly solitary, but after a few sessions, other children would join him, and he was able to give them directions to finding the 'best' sticks to use in the drumming area.

His final musical session was when he became the musical leader and instructed the whole group to make a musical recording. He ensured that everyone had their stick ready and were close together. He would conduct them to start or stop using different hand signals or voice commands.

C. was showing a 'musical intelligence' as described in the multiple intelligences devised by Howard Gardner (1983). One of the seven intelligences he lists is musical intelligence, which involves skill in performance, composition and appreciation of musical patterns. It allows a child to develop the capacity to recognise and compose musical pitches, tones and rhythms.

Initially C.'s sensory experiences were being enriched as his brain made new links with the sounds and the hand-eye co-ordination that was needed to make them. Over a period of time C. was able to develop his ability to create rhythms, sound patterns and beats and gained enough confidence in his own ability to involve other children and transfer this knowledge to them.

Making pitched instruments out of natural materials

A natural hanging xylophone can be made in any setting using materials collected from a forest or supplied by staff. You will need two lengths of rope and somewhere where you can suspend the instrument. Posts, trees, furniture or hooks in a wall can be used for this. In the case study below, the rope was long enough to reach between two adjacent trees. A horizontal xylophone can be made by using elastic bands to tie sections of wood together, starting with the shortest and gradually increasing the sizes as in a real xylophone.

CASE STUDY: MAKING A HANGING XYLOPHONE

The children had been talking about the crocodile and how he hadn't been feeling very well. (See Case Study in Chapter 1.) C suggested that he might like some music to cheer him up.

At the next session J. (adult) provided some sticks of different thickness and suggested they could make a xylophone. C. was eager to help and used a saw to help J. cut the branch into different lengths. J. used a length of rope and clove hitches to suspend the logs and then hung the rope between two trees. C. chose one of the spare logs to use as a beater. Initially she was unsure and only used the beater on two of the logs. With adult encouragement, she began to be more confident and experimented using all the log chimes. She then used two

beaters simultaneously and still using a simple beat and single notes moved between the chimes. She experimented using the beaters in a sideways movement between two suspended log chimes. She sustained this musical activity for half an hour on her own and became more imaginative as she composed different rhythm and sound patterns. She would compose a longer phrase and then repeat it. She also listened to an adult making sound patterns on another log and was able to copy those.

A Forest School xylophone

(J. adult and C. child)

This case study also highlights the role of the practitioner in planning and resourcing an activity based on a child's suggestion. This ensured that the child would understand and really engage in the activity.

Making shakers filled with natural materials

Children and adults can decide together what would make suitable containers. Strong cardboard tubes will give different sound patterns to plastic containers. Clear plastic tubes or bottles will enable children to create a shaker with different visual effects as well as different sound effects.

Children will enjoy collecting their own materials. In a non-forest setting adults may be able to bring in some collections of various items. Ideally the setting will have a rich supply of natural resources that is kept topped up and children may be able to select from these. Supply if possible: small stones, rounded pebbles, gravel, small and large twigs, different sized cones acorns, conkers, moss and leaves.

Making a shaker from natural materials

Experimenting with sounds outdoors using a variety of objects

Using instruments outdoors offers a much wider and more satisfying experience both for young children and adults. They are not restricted by having to play quietly so as not to disturb other activities in a classroom. If children do not access woodland on a regular basis, a dedicated music area can easily be made. The simplest way is to hang a line up and suspend different items from it. Provide sticks, beaters, or metal and wooden spoons for children to use.

Different provision for creating music and sound patterns

More sophisticated instruments can be made out of drain pipes, wooden pipes or guttering. Items commonly used are pots and pans. A frame can be made out of a wooden pallet or, if you want to achieve a natural look, use branches lashed together to make a frame and suspend your instruments from this. There are many ideas shown on Pinterest. Beaters need to be provided and keeping them in the right place may require some initial discussion with children.

Beaters are tied on to triangles and suspending them and the tambourines enables easy access for all children

Wooden spoons, spatulas or natural beaters made from twigs can be provided as a less expensive option. Tying fabric on some will give children a range of options as they experiment with the different sounds these make. Old cans, baking trays and metal pans are commonly used in an outdoor music area.

W. (16 months) had been given an old tin and after she had carried it round for a bit she dropped it on the decking at home. It made a resonant sound and she enjoyed this so much she dropped it again and again. Each time she stopped and carefully listened to the sound she was producing. She did this several times and then began to roll the tin, again enjoying the sound it made as it came into contact with hard wood.

This shows how an everyday item can help to develop children's listening skills as they experiment in their play

W. demonstrates a high level of concentration and also the ability to explore, experiment and think independently. When outside, she always responds to the sounds around her, a plane, machinery, traffic noise, the trees or bird calls. She stops what she is doing and looks around until she can, if possible, locate the source of the sound.

Making music with the body

Children can to be encouraged to use their own bodies to make music and sound patterns. Babies learn to clap their hands very often from an early age as they interact with an adult who may be holding their hands as they communicate with each other.

Many different rhythms can be achieved by using feet hands and arms to create different sound patterns. This can be extended outdoors by encouraging children to interact with natural materials. They can shuffle through leaves, stamp on them, tiptoe through them or jump off and on a piece of wood to create a rhythm pattern. Children can jump on and off logs and create pattern sequences. This activity can become very sophisticated when done by older children.

Using voices to create music

Singing to babies and young children from an early age is now known to have a profound effect on their subsequent ability to develop language and reading skills, but also contributes to their emotional well-being. Rocking and singing will soothe a tiny baby and singing nursery rhymes or making up silly songs helps to develop the bond between adult and child.

Many nursery settings use song and rhyme at the end of a session, but it is important to build these into the session itself, whether children are inside or outdoors. Very often a whole session will take place and children will not have been involved in any form of making music. Children will often sing as they play and it is important to note this and develop it.

Children may make up songs and with some adult encouragement can make up songs about just about anything. Forest School sessions around a campfire often use traditional campfire songs but children can be encouraged to make up their own words or music.

Singing songs around a campfire – one of the best ways of creating music outdoors

It is a good idea to start with a familiar tune and encourage children to make up words to fit the tune based on the experiences around them. This will help to develop their confidence and they may begin to create their own tunes as they sing. An example of this could be making up words to fit the tune 'The Wheels on the Bus'. Children could be sitting round their campfire and sing 'The smoke on the fire is swirling around, swirling around', etc. Or if they have been building a den: 'The side of the den is made with twigs, made with twigs', etc. followed by another verse, 'The roof of the den is built with ferns, built with ferns', and so on, with children making up their own verses as they go.

Encouraging children to respond creatively using instruments

Children need to have access to a range of pitched and unpitched instruments. There are many different types of drums available and children will begin to differentiate between sounds. Lucy, aged two and a half, was using a rain stick and said, 'Sounds like rain - swhooshes!'

Children may be able to use instruments as they move in different ways or they may use them to create different sound effects in a story. Initially, they may need to have experience of listening to an adult using instruments in this way, but they can soon become involved in this themselves and after a period of experimentation and discovery may begin to use instruments as part of their own story making and storytelling.

Using music and sounds to develop imaginative thinking

As children listen to the natural sounds of birdsong they will learn to distinguish different calls and sometimes even the range of calls from the same species. Adults can encourage children to think about why the bird is making that particular call. As children make their own shakers they can begin to use their imagination to answer the question 'What does it sound like?' or 'What does it remind you of?'

When children become more involved in imaginative themes in their play, music can be used to enhance the story line. They may produce a song for the fairies, create music for a dance, or compose some music for a dragon or a crocodile. Again, they may use instruments they have made or something provided by the adults. The key is to be creative in your own thinking as you decide how best to support the children's ideas.

Conclusion

Music has been held in high regard in societies and cultures from the earliest times. Today there are different evolving musical traditions and styles throughout the world. Musicians and composers are held in high esteem as they are the ones with the additional genius for composing and performing. Enjoying music whether listening or performing is one of the best ways to restore emotional calm and wellbeing. Learning to listen to the sounds around us helps us to become more aware of the world we live in. It tunes the ear and may offer emotional release as we listen to the natural sounds made by the waves, the wind rustling the leaves on a tree or the pebbles rolling around at the water's edge. It is important to help children learn to listen and to be aware of the sounds of nature. They will learn to hear the difference in tune and pitch as they experiment with sticks of different sizes and types. They will enjoy sharing their experiences with others, maybe using instruments or their voices. Music can be used to create special effects in stories and helps to develop children's own imagination and creativity.

POINTS FOR DISCUSSION

- Is music used throughout your sessions or just at the end? What can you do to create and encourage musical experiences of various types?

- How do you provide for children to make music outdoors? What can you do to extend this provision? Look at some of the ideas in the case studies.

- Is music used to enhance storytelling and encourage creative movement?

- Do you offer a range of instruments that reflect different cultures? Are children allowed to use these instruments outdoors?

- Can you make more use of natural resources to encourage children to make sounds and also make some instruments?

- Do you support children in their experiments with instruments or are they just 'left to get on with it'?

- Do you stop and listen to the sounds around us? How do you respond emotionally to what we hear?

- Are children encouraged to sing spontaneously? Are you as adults able to do this too?

- Think of ways you can involve families, maybe inviting them to a session to create instruments and sound patterns.

USEFUL RESOURCES

The Little Book of Garden Bird Songs by Andrea Pinnington and Caz Buckingham (Fine Feather Press 2015)

The Little Book of Woodland Bird Songs by Andrea Pinnington and Caz Buckingham (Fine Feather Press 2016)

Birdsong by Jonathan Elphick, Lars Svensson and Jan Pedersen (Quadrille Publishing Ltd. 2012)

Internet site: www.british-birdsongs.uk

National Trust guide to birdsong: https://www.nationaltrust.org.uk/features/our-guide-to-birdsong

The Listening Walk by Paul Showers (Harper Collins 1993)

The Ding Dong Bag by Polly Peters (Child'sPlay International 2006)

Ocean Drums and an exciting range of other percussion instruments can be bought online.

www.knockonwood.co.uk supply an inexpensive children's drum.

Collect clear plastic containers and a supply of natural objects to make shakers.

Bibliography

Armstrong, E.A. (1963) *A Study of Bird Song*. Oxford: Oxford University Press.
Gardner, H. (1983) *Frames of Mind*. New York: Basic Books.
Hartshorne, C. (1973) *Born to Sing*. Indianapolis: Indiana University Press.
Mathieu, W. (2011) *The Listening Book: Discovering your own Music*. Boulder: Shambhala Publications Inc.
Peery, J.C., Peery, I.C. and Draper, T.W. (1987) *Music and Child Development*. New York: Springer-Verlag.
Ransom, C.F. (1993) *Listening to Crickets – A Story about Rachel Carson*. Lerner Classroom.

9 Conclusion

In this chapter, we will briefly revisit what it means to be a creative teacher and a creative learner. The chapter summarises the role of the adult in supporting children's creativity and concludes by emphasising again the importance of letting children play outdoors on a daily basis. The term 'Creative Teaching' should be used in its widest sense to include all adults who are involved with young children whether they are parents, grandparents, relatives, carers or Early Years Practitioners.

The chapter reiterates:

- what it means to be a creative teacher

- the importance of developing secure emotional relationships with children

- the role of the adult in supporting children's own ideas and interests

- planning and resourcing spaces to encourage creativity outdoors

- ways to develop curiosity and imagination with particular reference to communication, building structures, listening and sound making, physical movement and colour, shape, form and pattern.

Creative teachers

Creative teachers will be keen to inspire their children to become creative learners. Being creative does not necessarily mean being able to draw or paint, compose music or design a building. It does mean however having the desire to further one's own learning. Becoming a creative learner is an important step towards being a creative teacher. It means being open minded and able to incorporate new ideas. 'It involves looking at familiar things with fresh eyes, examining problems with an open mind, making connections, learning from mistakes and using imagination to explore new possibilities' (Education Scotland 2013). This is a more recent definition of creativity but redefines the need expressed by Piaget earlier this century for educators to inspire children and enable them to become adults who:

> are capable of doing new things, not simply of repeating what other generations have done. … We need pupils who are active, who learn early to find out for themselves partly by their own spontaneous activity and partly by the materials we set up for them not to increase the amount of knowledge, but to create the possibilities for a child to invent and discover, to create people who are capable of doing new things.
>
> Piaget (1964) in Silberman (1973, p. xix)

Just playing and discovering

We need to become more aware of our own surroundings, making an effort to get outdoors ourselves, maybe examining how we actually feel about being outdoors. We need to open our eyes to what is around us, experience the wide open spaces of a beach or grassy field, a wide expanse of clouds and spend time watching a tiny insect scurrying across a garden or a woodland floor. Opening ourselves up to the natural environment in this way will enable us to support and extend the learning experiences of children in our care.

Young children may not have the same inhibitions as adults and we need to relax in our own bodies and become childlike again. Share the experiences of walking through a muddy puddle, throwing crunchy autumn leaves high in the air or playing with snow. Piaget reiterated this when he realised that adults need to retain something of their childhood and react spontaneously to situations in the way that young children do. We need to recognise the important of spontaneity and play. Children react instinctively to the world around them and want to explore and discover more. Through play they develop their imagination and curiosity. All their early learning is through play and discovery.

The more children are able to become involved in the deeper levels of play, the more they will be developing their capacity for concentration, emotional wellbeing and creative thinking. The way we react, respond, encourage and extend children's play is the key to developing creativity.

Adding a bowl for children to fill with water in a large sandpit extends play and children think and work as they create and solve problems

Relationships

Developing empathy and helping children to trust you are key factors in promoting wellbeing in young children. Some children need more support than others as they are separated from their parents maybe for the first time, to attend nursery. Phased visits and shorter sessions will help all children and the more anxious children may need sensitive intervention by practitioners. Some children may not be used to playing with others, either indoors or outdoors. Careful preparation is needed to support children in their first outdoor sessions whether in a nursery play space or a visit to the forest. A Forest School 'chatter box' can be used to help with this. This box might contain pictures, items previously found in woodland and some soft toys, e.g. a bird, an owl or a hedgehog.

A collection of items will encourage children to communicate about their feelings and experiences

As children grow in confidence, they will interact with other children as well as adults. Adults need to observe the children's interests and know when to intervene in a situation or when to step back. Children need to make their own discoveries, but a good practitioner will be able to challenge and extend children's learning. A good practitioner will respond to the interests of the child or group of children and plan to extend this. Creative planning will ensure children are able to be involved with activities over longer periods of time. Case studies in this book show this, and also how imaginative ideas can be passed on through the children themselves as they meet children who will be new to the setting.

CASE STUDY: THE ROLE OF THE ADULT

The adult is sharing this learning experience with the children

Gaining the trust of the children is an essential element of being able to be a successful Early Years practitioner. Once children trust you they will be willing to share and explore with you.

J. had introduced a collection of natural objects into a builder's tray in an urban nursery school setting. She then sat down at the table and began to explore the objects. Children immediately came to the area and were drawn into this journey of exploration. R. picked up a large shell and J. responded by picking up another one and holding it to her ear.

R. imitated this and then J. asked 'What can you hear?'

R. 'I hear a noise a noise, it's sort of shooshing, it's like the sea.'

Other children joined in and held shells to their ears.

D. 'I can't hear the sea — everyone's talking!'

J. 'Shall we be quiet together and then maybe you will?'

Another child L. showed an interest in J.'s camera and J. allowed him to take a picture of the group working together.

J. has responded by allowing L. to take a picture of the group

R. picked up a stick and used it to strike a stone. J. responded by using a stick on a piece of wood. This led to a discussion of different sounds made by the different objects.

R. placed some small stones on a piece of wood and picked up two sticks. He used the sticks as beaters and struck the stones. 'This is a xylophone.' J. listened as he made different sounds with the different sized stones.

R. has paused from playing his stone xylophone to watch A. building his tower

Children explored different objects and one held up a stone. 'This is stripy, it looks like ice cream.'

Immediately J. responded by holding it near her mouth. 'Yes it could be stone ice-cream'. Children laughed and joined in eating 'stone ice creams'.

A short while later, two boys played together to make small constructions, testing which small pieces of wood would stand up and stack. They added shells and sometimes fir cones to their structures. At one point, A. managed to stack five pieces of wood. It was tempting to ask how many he had stacked but after a short pause he looked at it and said 'I've used five pieces now'.

A. managed to stack five pieces of wood and was able to comment on this without any suggestions from the adult

Knowing when to ask questions and when not to, is an important skill. In this instance, the adult held back and the initiative came from the child, showing that he was already thinking in mathematical terms about his design. More than just counting, however, after some initial exploration and play he had selected the pieces according to size so the larger ones were at the bottom of the structure. This demonstrated his creativity in problem solving.

In this case study we see how just sharing and playing with children extends their concentration and interest. Some of these children had low levels of language and would have not engaged with the activity at all if J. had not sat at the table. She was able to direct the group but at the same time encourage and extend exploration. *At one point R. talks about the objects, points to shells, 'these go in water', then points to the rocks, 'rocks too in water, but these don't go in waters', pointing to large pine cones.*

J. asks 'Where do these come from?' 'These are pine cones. I see them when we go to the park, they grow on trees.' J. responded by saying, 'I am going to ask you to do a job for me. When you next see some in the park can you collect some and bring them into school for us to use?' Adults need to work with families and children to encourage them to help with resources.

Planning your space

Taking children outdoors every day is acknowledged to be part of good early years practice and we need creative adults to ensure that the spaces children use outdoors are exciting and challenging wherever the setting maybe. Some preschools need to pack away resources at the end of sessions and need to work out ways of transporting resources easily as well as providing pack away dens for children to use. Chapter 2 emphasises the importance of being creative as

This inviting den space was created at the back of a large flowerbed

you plan your outdoor space and suggests ways of developing it to offer a range of different learning opportunities. It will need the basic provision of sand and water, but think too about gravel and rockery areas, ropes and pulleys, areas for creative expression through music or dance. Creative use of plants such as bamboo, grasses or shrubs in pots can soften an outdoor area as well as providing materials for children to use in their play. Try to find an area for using different materials to make marks, and spaces for creating floor designs. There are many imaginative ideas on Pinterest.

If you are planning to develop your outdoor space, involve the parents and the local community. Be very clear about your aims and the benefits it will provide for the children. Local organisations and charities may be able to help with financial support. Some DIY stores may offer help with materials.

Resourcing your space

Once you have the basic layout in place, try to be creative about ways to use the spaces and remember to change things around occasionally. Creative resourcing is vital.

Children who attend Forest School will have access to a vast range of natural resources but even there, their creative problem solving will be enhanced by additional provision of various items.

Providing loose parts such as detailed in Chapter 2 is one of the easiest ways to encourage creative playing and learning. Jon Cree, a Director of the Forest School

Easy access to natural materials in an urban environment

Children helped to collect fallen twigs and leaves in this urban nursery and after watching an adult light a fire H. made his own 'pretend fire'

Association, says that it is perfectly possible to run Forest School in other environments through importing materials. Even if you do not have the capacity for providing the full Forest School ethos, hopefully you will be able to develop some of the ideas offered in this book.

A good resource base for children to use as they wish will enable them to become creative learners. Using natural materials is so important and children will develop their imagination as they imbue the items with different qualities. Collections of shells, conkers or pine cones can be used in so many ways. They will become the food on a spaceship, items in a shop, ingredients for a stew or decorations for sand or clay structures. Children will make potions out of flower petals and any other things that appeal to them.

Making potions – childhood memories are made from this

Many of us remember doing this and we need to ensure the next generation have a childhood that utilises the outdoor environment as much as possible. Be creative in your planning and resourcing. Extend your own thinking by looking at some recent research or articles online.

Developing children's curiosity and imagination

As children begin to engage with the spaces and resources you offer, they will begin to create their own scenarios and invent their own challenges and problems. It may be a practical task that requires some problem solving, such as in case study 'Moving the trolley' in Chapter 1. At Crosfield Nursery, Alexander wanted to sweep up the leaves but posed the question of what he should do with the leaves.

As shown in these photographs he decided to build a leaf store and solved the problem using blocks and an extra one to stand on so he could reach it.

It may be a more imaginative scenario such as building a home for the fairies, or feeding the crocodile in the woods. Adults need to observe closely the way children interact with the environment and with each other. They need to note the conversations and plan how to extend the children's interests. The creative use of provocations as discussed in Chapter 4 will offer opportunities for open ended discussion, rich opportunities to develop language and possible action. Children will be experiencing 'possibility thinking', as defined by Anna Craft and discussed in Chapter 1.

Developing creative communication

Creative teachers will use creative language as they share experiences with children. They will describe the shades of green, the colours of autumn and the sensory experiences of being in a garden space or in the woods. Use adjectives as you talk about things the children find. They will learn new vocabulary only by hearing new words and using them for themselves. Involve children in storytelling and story making. Research some traditional tales and use those as well as more familiar stories. Share poetry with children, encouraging them to string words together. Children will often do this naturally in their language experiments and create poetic strings. It is through language that children's thought patterns develop and their problem solving skills emerge. Encourage children to use reference books, technology and photographs related to their interests to encourage and inspire them in their creative expression, whether it be through language, music or working with colour and form. Listening to children and giving them space and time to express their thoughts and ideas is crucial. Children also need the confidence to talk to each other and to share their ideas. Social skills will develop too as they begin to work together, maybe developing one of their ideas. Small inviting spaces in the outdoor setting can encourage conversations and children may use a slightly larger space to re-enact a story that they have heard. Children can enjoy the physical challenge of creating their own spaces and these in turn lead to complex role-play scenarios, where children take on roles, make their own rules and act out various situations.

Developing creative structures

Creative teachers will understand the thrill of making a den and having a private space. They may have experienced this as children themselves, but they will want to provide the materials and encourage children to do this. They will also begin to explore possibilities of using natural materials in many different ways with children. They will follow the children's interests and encourage them to have their own ideas. Large structures may involve children learning safe ways to carry long sticks, and then how to balance them safely so they do not fall and hurt someone. Direct teaching following the safety points in Chapter 5 will give guidance here. Children can use natural materials in so many ways and begin to understand elements of design and construction. Large scale den building is one of the most popular of childhood activities and dens feature now in many outdoor spaces such as National Trust properties, RHS gardens and city parks.

Smaller structures too encourage children to think imaginatively, as they plan a party for the fairies, or mix medicine for the crocodile. They have an amazing capacity for using whatever they find and imbuing their treasures with characteristics that fit in with their imaginative play. When out in the woods or on a beach children can become deeply involved as they build from sand or wood, decorate with feathers acorns, shells or seaweed. Their imagination knows no bounds and a supportive adult will visit their shop or ride in their train, eat from the cafe or join in the tea party for the fairies or woodland animals.

Many public spaces now offer den making facilities – encourage families to use these!

Developing opportunities for creative movement

Forest School offers safe risk taking and challenge. Children have opportunities for physical development in so many more ways when they are outside. If they can run, climb and jump, walk over different surfaces, dodge through brambles and step over fallen branches, they will be developing many more muscles than they can possibly do indoors. Many children live in flats which are accessed by lifts and by the age of three, some children have not developed the skill of climbing stairs. Any outdoor space, therefore, needs to be carefully planned to offer the maximum opportunity for physical development. Building in mounds, slopes or stairways will help and different textures on the ground can offer different challenges.

This raised rope space was created in the corner where the old shed used to be

Using some of the ideas from Forest School and some of the natural materials such as logs, stumps, tree trunks and branches offers children some interaction with natural elements. These present so many more interesting challenges than manmade, uniformly constructed climbing frames and balance bars. Strong physical movement develops the muscles and the brain and increases coordination and control. This in turn enables children to be confident in their approach to challenges. They need to think about how they can move safely as each log or tree is different. Risk taking becomes part of adventurous outdoor play and creative practitioners will know how to complete appropriate risk assessments. They will use positive language to encourage children as they climb, crawl or balance safely and develop their physical strength and confidence.

Creative movement can be encouraged as children gain more control of their bodies. A combination of music, sound patterns and rhythms may inspire children to respond with different movement styles. Children may observe natural phenomena and build these into their creative responses through movement and dance. They may sway like the wind or move like different creatures they have observed in their outdoor spaces. They love to wriggle along like worms, crawl like a humpy caterpillar or jump like baby frogs.

Jumping like baby frogs

Developing sound making and music outdoors

Creative teachers will offer music to children in a variety of ways. Songs, rhythms and music will be built into the sessions whether indoors or outdoors. Children will learn to listen to the sounds around them and may even respond with their own voices or an instrument. They can make a range of instruments using natural resources and experiment with sound patterns without it interfering with nearby activities. There is so much more opportunity for experimenting with sound outdoors. Children can work on their own or together with their peers. Musical creativity should be valued as much as artistic creativity and children may be able to develop their understanding of tone and rhythm simply using different types of wood on different surfaces outdoors.

Interacting with the colours, shapes, patterns and forms of the natural world

Natural resources can inspire a whole range of creativity and the colours and textures of different objects are used in many ways as children set them out in patterns, often making definite choices about shape and colour. They may use clay to add dimension and form, such as shown in the case study in Chapter 7 where they created creatures as part of the story of Mother Earth. Mixing potions, using paint, charcoal and other natural elements are all ways of extending the creativity of young children and if this can happen in an outdoor space, there is far more scope for creations to be left untouched so children can revisit them over time. This book has deliberately not included ideas for structured 'art' activities. Through observation and exploration, it is hoped that children and adults will become excited by the natural world around them. This will inspire ideas as children play and explore materials, colours, textures and forms. A rotting tree stump may look like a dinosaur or other imaginary creature and children can explore the textures and develop their imaginations as they climb on such a tree trunk.

Look out for interesting natural forms which children can explore

A creative teacher will be inspired and encourage children to observe and explore. In addition, there should be high quality provision of a range of media to encourage children to create and recreate in a variety of ways. Children will also enjoy using cameras to capture some of the shapes and forms they find.

Conclusion

Play is the way that young children learn and the more imaginative their play becomes, the more chance they will have of developing the life skills they will need. The competition for jobs is increasing; employers are beginning to look for people who are able to motivate others, to inspire, to offer solutions and ways forward.

We need to take our children outside every day to help them develop an awareness of the world around them, have respect and care for the natural world and to offer experiences that are challenging and fun. We need to encourage them to discover for themselves. We need to give them the opportunity to make decisions, to invent their games, and work with their peers, establishing rules and following different lines of enquiry.

In 2017 the International School Grounds Alliance published a declaration stating that 'School grounds should not be as safe as possible but as safe as necessary'. The declaration cites research from around the worlds which demonstrated the benefits of risk taking and how indiscriminate risk minimisation policy can be a source of harm. 'Since the world is full of risks, children need to learn to recognise and respond to them in order to protect themselves and to develop their own risk assessment capabilities.'

Forest School practitioners are trained to understand this and to encourage children to recognise risks and respond appropriately. If all early years practitioners were able to receive this training then some of our settings would be very different places. There would be less green or grey safety surface, and hopefully not nearly so many plastic ride-on toys or fixed climbing frames. Children would be offered a range of materials so they could invent and construct for themselves.

The more they discover, the more they will want to discover and as their imagination develops so the skills of possibility thinking need to be understood and developed. In order to be creative we need to be open to new ideas, sensations and processes. We need to know how to respond to these and to have time to reflect on our responses. Michael Rosen discusses this in the foreword to Born Creative, and emphasises the organisational role of the leader. There should be sensitivity to difference and a sense of democracy. The lines of communication within the group should not just pass between the leader and the individuals in the group – there need to be as many lines sideways between the participants. He stresses too that there needs to be a sense that there are many ways of getting things 'right' rather than a definitive right or wrong. There should be a shared interest in the process. Creativity also requires time for people to reflect on that

The natural curiosity of toddlers needs to be safely supported and encouraged

production or process: 'None of this is a luxury. It is essential for the advance of humankind.' Creative learning involves investigating, discovering, inventing and cooperating. Rosen (2010) says at least one of these will be present in any creative learning experiences. Ideally it will be all four.

You may decide to complete Forest School training and hopefully find ways of using these skills even in an urban nursery or one with limited space. Take inspiration from the natural world. Look at the patterns in stones, on the skins of creatures and the feathers of birds. Marvel at the intricacy of a leaf structure or a spider's web glistening in the autumn sunlight. Awaken in yourself the creative spirit which will enable you to encourage and inspire the children in your care.

It is the supreme art of the teacher to awaken joy in creative expression and knowledge.
(Albert Einstein in Calaprice 2011, p. 101)

Time for reflection!

FINAL POINTS FOR DISCUSSION

■ Consider the role of the adult in the case study in this chapter. How does she respond to different needs and interests of individual children? Examine the way she interacts with children. What are the children learning?

■ How creative is your language when you speak to children? Are you including new and exciting words for them to hear?

■ Consider how you can improve your outdoor environment. Are you able to offer some more adventurous activities for children?

■ Can you look objectively at your outdoor space with reference to this book and create an action plan to change and develop it, maybe looking at each area of creativity in turn?

Bibliography

Calaprice, A. (2011) *The Ultimate Quotable Einstein*. Princeton: Princeton University Press.

Education Scotland (2013) *Creativity across Learning 3–18*. Available at: https://education.gov. scot/improvement/Documents/Creativity/CRE1_WhatAreCreativitySkills/Creativity3to18.pdf.

International School Grounds Alliance (2017) *Risk in Play and Learning: Ubud-Höör Declaration*. Available at: www.internationalschoolgrounds.org/risk.

Rosen, M. (2010) Foreword, in C. Tims (ed.), *Born Creative*. Available online at https://www.demos. co.uk/project/born-creative/.

Silberman, C.E. (1973) *The Open Classroom Reader*. New York: Random House.

Index

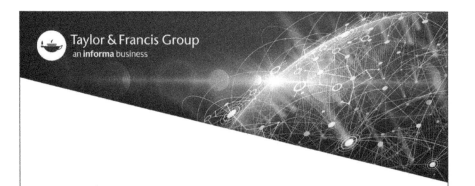